It Shouldn't Happen to a Methodist Minister

Leslie Marsh

Copyright © Leslie Marsh 2024

All rights reserved

ISBN: 9798320783185

In memory of Barbara, my wife, for whom Jesus came first

I find God occasionally works through me, but generally without me – and mostly in spite of me.

– *Rajmohan Gandhi, a grandson of the Mahatma*

When I was born an English man
Each other race was an also ran.
They did their best to play the game,
But they never quite made it just the same.
They naturally wanted to be like me,
But we kept them in their places and we ruled the sea.

– *The herald's song in 'The Vanishing Island' by Peter Howard*

Contents

Preface . . . . *vii*

1. A family 'business' 1
2. Does God exist? 8
3. Apprenticeship in living my faith. 17
4. Training for the ministry. 24
5. Winning the Communists 29
6. Theatrical ventures. 34
7. Britain's first theatre-church 42
8. Better than a thousand sermons 48
9. John Wesley takes to the stage 55
10. Challenging apartheid. 59
11. *Ride! Ride!* goes national. 65
12. Mental illness 70
13. An unlikely setting for musical prowess. 73
14. A cure to corruption 77
15. A church transformed. 85
16. A transformative new perspective. 89
17. A tragic event 96
19. An author at 85. 99

Preface

What is the role of a church minister? It has taken me into areas of life far beyond what I expected when I started in my first circuit in Yorkshire.

I come from a line of Methodist ministers, and have served widely in England's industrial heartland, in Wales and in southern England. Amidst the traditional role of a minister, I have found myself involved in expressing the truths of Christianity through theatre and in other unusual ways. I have worked with militant trade union leaders and with business executives, and have seen these truths resolve conflict in difficult industrial and political situations.

I kept no diaries and hardly any records, so I have just written of things I remember. Memory plays tricks but in all that matters I believe my account is accurate. In one case I've substituted 'Ernie' for a name I can't remember.

I leave out my routine work of a minister's day. When I started as a Local Preacher in the 1940s a minister's work was seen as a morning preparing sermons, an afternoon visiting the sick, taking women's meetings and caring for his (we were all 'his' then) congregations. Business meetings took up the evening.

At the turn of the 20th century, when everyone still walked, a distant relation of mine was my predecessor in North Cave and took the quarterly trustees meetings at Broomfleet, a church on the Humber river eight miles away. He often took his wife and she spent the evening with the wife of the trust secretary.

Once when the trustees' meeting ended about 10 pm – with his mind perhaps full of some difficult business – he set off for home. Arriving home at midnight, no light on reminded him that he'd forgotten his wife. He had to walk back the eight miles, arriving to pick her up at 2 am. A lady who knew her said that he wouldn't have had a dull moment on his walk with her all the way home.

My father had a similar misfortune. He was minister in Blackpool when he married. After every Sunday evening service he went for a walk with the church steward along the cliffs. The Sunday after his marriage he forgot that his wife was waiting for him in the church porch and went off with the steward for his usual walk. I do not know what happened on his return, but I understand he never forgot again.

I never faced such a problem when I married, as the manse was but a few doors from the church. But I now realise I was too often as insensitive as my forebears. However, despite all my failings, and thanks to so many people, most of all my wife, I have had a fascinating life. I leave you to judge what (if any of it?) was God's doing.

1
A family 'business'

There were few jobs where my grandfather Arthur was born, one of nine sons of an East Anglian farm labourer in West Wratting, Suffolk. He walked to Cambridge for work, and started a small painting and decorating business. He and his wife Caroline had five children and the youngest was my father, Herbert George. When Herbert was aged 4, my grandfather, who had been ill, fell off a ladder and died, leaving my grandmother with their five young children.

Normally the children would have been put in the workhouse, but Caroline fought like a tigress to keep her family together, and took on a small butchering business.

Arthur and Caroline Marsh with their family c 1891: (l to r) Arthur, Henry, Herbert, Lottie, Percy.

It Shouldn't Happen to a Methodist Minister

The family belonged to the Primitive Methodist church, which one historian calls:

> … a working class movement which gave its adherents a sense of self-worth and a desire for improvement. Its chapels provided education and an opportunity to develop skills in public speaking and leadership. It also provided an alternative way of life, based on moral values, which helped raise families out of poverty.

The chapel was the centre of Arthur and Caroline's lives. Arthur was a Local (lay) Preacher, but today the largest monument on the wall in their church is to Caroline. Three of their sons became Methodist ministers, and the fourth, Percy, gave lifelong service to Castle Street Methodist church – apart from a few years when he served as pastor of a Primitive Methodist church in Scotland.

The family lived at the castle end of Cambridge at 8 and 9 Northampton Street. The houses were opposite Kettle's Yard, then regarded as the most notorious slum in Cambridge, but now a highly regarded estate. They had one valuable possession – a tablecloth which came out once a week for Sunday lunch. Disaster struck when one day an aunt from next door, an alcoholic, stole and pawned it. Caroline went to the pawn shop and got it back. The incident gave Herbert a life-long anger towards the alcohol trade, and in adulthood he fought the trade by opposing all licence applications – and usually winning.

As a child he joined in all the games in the street. One of them involved daring each other to see who could lean out furthest over the bridge. Herbert won, and the white mark of the cut on his forehead – caused when his head hit the ground below the bridge – remained throughout his life. He also had a finger crushed when helping his mother mangle the clothes on wash day.

Herbert taught himself to read from his father's Local Preacher's books in the attic, and he excelled. He was the first pupil his castle-end school put up for the scholarship to the Perse School, a private school with a high reputation for academic achievement.

On the appropriate day, the Perse School hall filled with boys applying for the scholarship and the tall, fearsome-looking headmaster came onto the platform with a large book. Opening it, he gave it to the first boy on the front row to read out, then pass it on.

All read with some difficulty until it came to my father, a very small boy. He chirped it out merrily until the head shouted 'Stop! You've read this before,' implying cheating. 'No sir,' the petrified boy replied. 'We'll soon see,' said the head, who stamped off to his office. Reappearing with a copy of that morning's *Times*, and opening it at the leading article, he handed it to my father saying, 'Read that.' To the head's astonishment, my father duly did so and the scholarship was his.

At first he was welcomed by the other boys, but his poverty was clear from his trousers, which his mother had made out of all she had, her petticoat. Soon one after another came and said their parents had told them they must have nothing to do with him. This caused him to play truant, until his uncle, a shop assistant in the town's leading department store, Eaden Lilley, bought him a proper pair.

A brilliant classics teacher, WHS Jones of St Catharine's College, Cambridge, saw Herbert's ability and encouraged him, with the result that he won an open exhibition in history to the college, and went on to gain his Master's degree there.

He intended to become a minister, but in those days Cambridge theology was closed to ministerial training for the Primitive Methodists. So he went to Manchester and

It Shouldn't Happen to a Methodist Minister

St Catharine's College, Cambridge

gained a first in his Bachelor of Divinity degree, completing the three-year course in two years. Later he was awarded a Doctor of Divinity for his work on baptism and became a revered church theologian.

A degree wasn't always highly regarded by his fellow 'Prims' (as the Primitive Methodists were known). Going to his first church, he was met at the railway station by the circuit steward, the leading layman in a group of Primitive churches. 'We hear you've got a degree?' asked the steward. 'Yes,' Herbert humbly admitted. 'Well, we won't hold it against you,' said the steward.

Two years later the minister of Castle Street was elected President of the Primitive Methodist Church, and Herbert moved to Cambridge to take charge of the church for the year the minister would be away. One Sunday after evening service, Herbert and Percy were standing in the porch of the church when a Catholic lad went by offering some 'cheeky' advice. Percy grabbed the boy and gave him a whack. The howling youngster went down the hill to tell his mother in the pub, and a swarm of angry Irish women emerged from the pub. Percy just had time to escape out of the back door of the church as the swarm flew in at the front. Ecumenical relations had yet to develop in those days.

Along with my father, my maternal grandfather, three uncles and a cousin were all Primitive Methodist ministers and my maternal aunt a deaconess. At my baptism my adopted grandmother declared, 'Our Leslie's going to be a preacher like his father.' When I was of age, being a shrewd businesswoman she pressed me instead to 'be a doctor, then you can both do good and make money'. But by then it was too late. I had already decided.

Herbert Marsh, Leslie's father, in the 1920s

Leslie aged 3 with Dad

Despite being the son of a minister, I wasn't a good little boy. I liked fighting, told lies when necessary or to impress, and once on an impulse stole a toy cannon from a shop. At school we all claimed 'My Dad can fight your Dad.' My Dad was a small man who wouldn't hurt a flea, but that made no difference.

I had just turned five when my father moved to a new church in Manchester. After his first service, the leading ladies gathered in the porch eager to meet my mother Beryl and her children. I was introduced to the leading layman's son, aged six. 'This is Sidney,' my mother said. 'I'll fight you,' I said to Sidney, just to open our conversation like. 'I don't fight on Sundays,' replied Sidney. 'Well I do,' I said, giving him an uppercut that laid him flat on his back across the church porch. I don't remember being punished for this. My mother, recounting the story to me years later, gave me the impression that she had been quite amused at this evidence that I could stand up for myself.

One day when I was nearly seven, a twelve-month-old baby arrived. She was lying back in a pram in the kitchen. Her name was Ruth, I was told, and my parents had adopted her. I remember my mother being keen to assure me that I would always be special, but I couldn't see a baby as competition anyway.

At school I had recently learnt to do sums. So I set up my blackboard, which I'd probably been given for Christmas, in front of her pram and wrote on it, '1 + 1 = 2'. I turned round to find my new little sister immersed in laughter. As I moved to 'teach her a lesson' my mother intervened, saying, 'She's only a baby'. I didn't think this was any excuse, but it ended my interest in my baby sister for some time.

Ruth, as she grew up, was warm-hearted to all, but was found to have limited abilities. She lived with my parents until they died, and worked as a shop assistant.

2
Does God exist?

I was born into an age of British imperialism. My father could remember the fireworks in Cambridge to celebrate the relief of Mafeking during the Boer war. The British Empire extended across much of the world, and its influence extended even further. Though China was never part of the empire, for many years the Chinese government would not act against the wishes of the British Resident in Shanghai. Everyone I saw was white and English.

A history book in my school library said an Englishman was worth 'three dagos (Southern Europeans) or ten natives (darker-skinned races)'. I imbibed the idea that we English were a superior race, and thought of Manchester where I lived as the greatest city in the world. Aged six or seven I enjoyed singing with other kids as we played in the street:

> Won't you come to Abyssinia won't you come.
> Bring your own ammunition and a gun.
> Mussolini will be there,
> Shooting peanuts in the air…

and to Walt Disney's tuneful Snow White:

> Whistle while you work
> Mussolini is a twerp,
> Hitler's barmy,
> So's his army…

After the war had started we sang:

> We're going to hang out our washing on the Siegfried line,
> Have you any dirty washing mother dear…

Leslie Marsh

When I was eight I heard some women in the street talking anxiously of war. I didn't know what war meant, but I was worried until the greengrocer who sold bananas joined in the conversation, firmly saying, 'There won't be a war.' My anxiety vanished.

One day when I was nine my Dad said, 'Come and listen to this. You'll always remember it.' The radio went silent, and then a voice came on: '… we have received no such assurance… we are at war with Germany.' A night or so later I was awakened by the scary wail of the air raid siren and my panic-stricken mother rushing in to get me down into the dank cold cellar which was our air raid shelter. It was a false alarm and the 'all clear' siren soon went. We returned to bed.

We were the end house of the row and our cellar was the shelter for the whole row, so it was soon made comfortable with its own coal fire. My pals lived a couple of doors away. When air raids became frequent we looked forward to them as we could play with our toys instead of going to bed. When Manchester was blitzed at Christmastime 1940, my father, an air raid warden watching for fire bombs, came down saying Manchester was like one great bonfire lighting up the whole sky. It sounded much like bonfire night and I was extremely disappointed not to be allowed up from the cellar to see it.

At the start of the war my school was closed, so I lost a year's schooling. The outlook was very uncertain so my father decided to send me to Kingswood, a Methodist boarding school for ministers' sons in Bath, founded in the eighteenth century. At that time John Wesley moved ministers to a different area every fortnight, because they had to have something interesting enough to keep people awake for an hour at five o'clock each morning, and Wesley thought they couldn't do that for more than a fortnight.

It Shouldn't Happen to a Methodist Minister

Kingswood School enabled their children to have an uninterrupted education, thanks to charitable grants.

The Kingswood preparatory school, where I started, had been evacuated to the country home of the biscuit maker Huntley and Palmer near Chieveley in Berkshire. The first night in our dormitory the new boys were crying from homesickness. I didn't feel homesick and felt very superior. By the second night I was homesick and couldn't now admit it. So I said I was thirsty because I couldn't drink the water. They'll surely have to send me home, I thought. It didn't work and I was left to sob my way to sleep. By the time we got up the next morning my aversion to the water had strangely evaporated.

My first term I didn't over-work and had been moved down from the 3rd to the 4th form. My grades in the end of term report were all 'C's. My father threatened that my world would end if they weren't all 'A's in future. From then on I did all I could to get 'A's.

I liked to be noticed. When one boy asked if any of us were afraid of spiders and all said 'no', I got their attention by saying 'yes', though in fact I had no problem. Bertie Bellis caught a spider and led a lynch mob to make me eat it. I was barely average height but I had unusual strength and I could look after myself. He beat a quick retreat with a bloody nose and the mob rapidly vanished. The headmaster also seemed pleased with the outcome.

When I was 13 I moved to the senior school, which had been evacuated to share the buildings of Uppingham School. In my first year my class performed a play. I hoped for the leading role but was given the part of 'second Roman soldier'. I had to enter, say 'Yes sir', and exit. Disgruntled, I protested by coming onto the stage late, 'forgetting' to take my glasses off – which raised laughter at the wrong point – 'forgot' my words and had to be prompted; then 'forgot' to exit, needing another prompt. I was never given a part again. At least this was not a national news story, unlike my second theatrical entry twenty years later.

By the time I reached my teens I thought the answer for the world was Christianity and the British Empire which, seen through my 'rose-tinted spectacles', would bring justice, peace, and trains everywhere. I asked my teacher whether Holland might join the British Empire after the war – to the derision of my classmates. He was a wise teacher and sheltered me from the derision. As for the war I never had any doubt that we would win – my father said, 'England always loses every battle, except the last' – and mostly the war was far from my thoughts. No one I knew was involved in actual fighting and the reports I heard were always positive.

At my baptism my grandmother had declared I'd be a minister 'like my Dad', and all my relatives thought the same. To follow one's father was still a fashion and I accepted I'd be a minister. Everybody loved my father and he did good to people. I wanted to be loved and 'do good to people'. I liked speaking and thought I was good at it. But I had a problem: was there a God? My father and mother believed in God. If I didn't know whether God existed I'd be like a vegan in a butcher's shop. I skimmed all the philosophy books in the library in a search for 'proof', and began arguing with everybody, making myself more and more unpopular.

My mother's mother had died when my mother was only six years old and her father married the woman who had nursed her. My mother never got on with her step-mother. When she was 16, she asked her father to let her go and live with Mr and Mrs Coombs, a couple who had built the most fashionable 'department' store in Northwich, as they needed a home help. Her father agreed. Her relationship with her father must have worsened, as she changed her name to Coombs and married under that name without telling her father. When he found out he stormed into the J W Coombs department store, accusing them of stealing his daughter. It made a scandalous public scene in the town.

I didn't know I had another grandfather until my eleventh birthday, when my natural grandfather sent me a present via my parents. I was boarding at Kingswood prep school and my father typed me a careful letter of thanks for me to send, asking me to copy it out 'word for word'. I thought that was too much trouble and simply crossed through my typed signature, signed 'Leslie' and posted it in the envelope my father had prepared. My parents were puzzled that they hadn't heard again from my natural granddad and when I came home they quizzed me. I happily confessed what I had done, thinking it very clever. It received a pained gasp as my father groaned to my mother, 'That's why we haven't heard'.

My laziness dashed hopes of healing the relationship for another ten years, and I was in my twenties when, with Grandma Coombs' agreement, I was sent across the Pennines to meet granddad Didcock. He was a retired Methodist minister living in a care home. He was also a Fellow of the Royal Astronomical Society. In his earlier days he had gone to prison for taking part in a campaign to end the practice whereby non-conformists (Methodists and others) had to pay tithes to support Church of England vicars.

My adopted grandfather Coombs' worldview was formed in the violent struggles between Irish immigrant Catholics and English Protestants in Liverpool at the start of the twentieth century. He indoctrinated me with anti-Catholic propaganda. Though Hitler had conquered Europe, for me the Pope was a worse enemy. We had a brilliant English teacher, an Anglican, who asked us for an

My grandparents Joseph and Harriet Williams Coombs. Behind them (l to r) my parents Beryl and Herbert, and my sister Ruth

essay each week on any subject we chose. From me he got one every week on the papal menace. Four weeks before my school certificate exams he declared me 'unteachable' and said he wouldn't have me in his class. I got a wry look from him when my school certificate results came through. I had gained distinction in both English language and English literature. He had taught me more than enough without my realising it.

An older cousin used to send me a 'good' book, normally a classic, for birthdays and Christmas. I dutifully wrote to thank him but never read them. On my 17th birthday he sent me a book and I made my usual reply. A month later he called by unexpectedly, and asked me what I thought of the book. I said it was 'all right'. He was obviously astonished by my answer, so I explained that I hadn't 'quite finished it' – which was true, though I hadn't quite begun it either. 'How could I begin it without finishing it?' he asked, causing me an urgent prolonged trip to the bathroom till he'd gone. But as he planned to call again I thought I'd have to read it.

It Shouldn't Happen to a Methodist Minister

It was by Peter Howard, a brilliant political journalist who wrote for the *Daily Express*, the largest and most influential paper of the day. He was feared by many politicians thanks to his skill at exposing their failings. Though he had been born with a lame leg, he rose to captain England at rugby and won a gold medal in the Winter Olympics for bobsleighing.

After Lord Beaverbrook, owner of the *Daily Express*, joined Churchill's Cabinet, Howard's articles attacking Beaverbrook's cabinet colleagues proved embarrassing and he was banned from political writing. Seeking other targets he hit upon the Oxford Group, a prominent Christian movement in the 1930s led largely by former Oxford students. It was now beginning to be called Moral Re-Armament, MRA, and a false smear that they were pro-Nazi had made them controversial. (Since 2000 it has been known as Initiatives of Change.)

Howard went to meet Garth Lean, a member of the Oxford Group. When Garth mentioned God, Howard interrupted with, 'I don't believe in God.' Garth's response was to suggest to Peter that he might make an experiment. 'Get up a little earlier one morning, sit quietly asking God to speak to you, and write down all the thoughts that come

Peter Howard at the Daily Express

to you – on the understanding that you will carry out any thought that's in line with Christ's standards of honesty, purity, unselfishness, and love.' Thinking this would make a good article, 'How I listened to God' (ha! ha!), the next morning Peter did just that. To his surprise, thoughts came which, when he implemented them, transformed his life.

Reading his story, I wanted what he'd found. One morning I got up a quarter of an hour earlier and made the experiment. When I thought about those four standards of absolute honesty, purity, unselfishness and love, many things swept into my mind which I wrote down – some of things I'd long forgotten. I decided to carry out all these thoughts.

I returned money to a bookshop whose short-sighted shop assistant had undercharged me; made restitution to a boy whose orange I had stolen; asked forgiveness for talking about a younger boy I was jealous of behind his back; told my sister that I would never hit her with a walking stick again; and, most difficult of all, told my house-master, Mr Sedge, that I had lied in explaining why I had a packet of cigarettes.

Sedge had a cane known as 'Whistling Willie' because when he caned a boy, the cane came down so fast it whistled. I had bought the cigarettes to smoke going home when term ended, but I had told Sedge that I'd bought them as an Easter present for my father. He told me to go and get the packet. Fortunately I hadn't opened it. He took it and returned it to me at the end of term and I gave it to my father. My father was pleased with my kind thought but pointed out that he didn't smoke. That ended for me the attraction of cigarettes.

Somehow I was given the strength to do these things, and from that moment God became real to me. I suddenly saw with new eyes that I was the same as everyone else and, for the first time, was really interested in others. Walking down a corridor I felt I was walking on air. I only felt the ground under my feet again as I turned the corner to my dayroom. It was as if a great load I didn't even know I was carrying had fallen off my back.

I realised that I'd been fearful of leaving school. Now I knew that God had a plan for me and everyone. People who had kept well away now wanted to find out what had happened to me.

I was the one sixth-former who had not been made a prefect. Seeing the change, 'Sedge' made me a prefect. This meant I had to take my turn in supervising the juniors when they did their 'prep' (homework) of an evening.

Twenty years later, getting off a train in Crewe, I bumped into a man I recognised as one of the juniors I'd supervised. 'Didn't I take you for prep at KS?' I asked. 'Yes,' he replied, 'and you were the only sane one among them.' This was added confirmation that I did not just feel different. My whole behaviour had changed.

3
Apprenticeship in living my faith

From school I was fortunate enough to win the same open exhibition in history to St Catharine's College, Cambridge as my father. In 1908 the £60 award had paid my father's fees to the college, but in 1950 the government paid all fees and maintenance. I left school a term early to do my national service in the army. I was allocated to the Royal Signals.

National Service, Catterick Camp

National service normally lasted two years. But as the universities wanted their students to start their courses when the university year began, the Government agreed that people going on to university would only have to do 18 months. When the Korean war started, the Government stopped the scheme. But it stood for those who had already been accepted to university.

I was selected for officer training. As well as basic military training we were taught wireless and telegraphy and its practical application. As I had done no science at school I found this useful, and I learnt to repair telephones and wirelesses.

The six weeks' infantry training ended with an exhausting 24-hour exercise. We arrived back in our dormitory having had no sleep, and all agreed that no way could we clean up properly for the parade an hour later. The captain inspected the parade. 'Mr Blank,' he said to the first cadet in shocked tones, 'your brasses are dirty.' 'Yes sir,' came the reply in correct military manner. And so to the next cadet, getting the same response.

As he moved to me, someone on the back row tittered and I lost control, grinning all over my face. 'Mr Marsh,' I heard him saying, 'control yourself.' But I couldn't. The parade was cancelled and I was ordered to do the whole course again for 'an unmilitary outlook on the army'. This gave insufficient time to post me to Korea on completion of my training. Instead, after commissioning, I was kept in this country in charge of a troop managing telephone lines.

After my national service I arrived in Cambridge and joined the small team of students whose lives had been transformed like mine. Our little team included Tony, a university rowing champion, Guy, an agriculturalist from Kenya, Frank, who was also studying agriculture, and several others. Each of our team rose for an hour's quiet reflection at six o'clock every morning – a revolutionary action for students in Cambridge at that time – and met each day at 7.30 am to share the thoughts that had come to us.

At that time Communism seemed to be taking over the world – already all Eastern Europe and China had fallen, with Italy, France and West Germany on the brink – and many people thought that we would soon have to choose between dictatorship and an atomic war that would destroy everyone.

We offered a third way – a new world where unselfishness replaced selfishness, honesty and integrity ended corruption, purity answered destructive relationships and broken marriages, and genuine love brought fair economic and political solutions.

The only other students with a vision for the world and dedicated to changing it were the Communists. We set out to get to know them. One Communist party member with whom I became friends was engaged in party activity throughout the day. He studied when everyone had gone to bed between eleven at night and three in the morning.

We decided to hold a meeting in the University Union, and invited a group of young men and women active with MRA in Britain, including people from other countries. We also invited Tom Keep, President of the National Stevedores and

Tom Keep

Dockers Union, who formerly had been a Communist but had decided that MRA was a better way to bring change.

A large audience turned out to hear them, and their attention was held by the experiences related from the stage. Soon after Tom Keep got up to speak, the Communist students turned out the lights. Tom was used to such tactics and carried on speaking as if nothing had happened. Before he'd finished we'd managed to get the lights back on.

After this a student called Brian Lightowler asked if he could join us, and we invited him to our 7.30 am meeting the next morning. We had decided to concentrate on 'love', so we suggested that he read 1 Corinthians 13. His King James Bible translated the Greek 'love' as 'charity' and next morning a very puzzled Brian arrived saying he couldn't find anything about love in that passage. This was his start to an amazing life that led, among much else, to 'clean election campaigns' which have helped to curb bribery in national elections on three continents – as I describe in Chapter 14.

At that time racism was taken for granted in England. Each year Cambridge students held a rag week to raise money for charity, and in my first year they decided to hold a 'slave market'. Guy Grant came from Kenya, a country soon to be immersed in the Mau Mau uprising against British rule. His father had been murdered by a Kenyan spear, and he educated our team about African feelings. Although the preparations for the slave market had been made, he went and talked to the committee and the whole idea was quietly scrapped.

Experiences like this radically modified my idea that the British Empire and Western ideas of Christianity were the answer for the world though, looking back now, much unrecognised racism remained in me. I hadn't even understood what 'racism' was.

Leslie Marsh

As the end to my time at Cambridge approached I had to decide whether to offer for the ministry. By then I realised that my motives for going into the ministry had been all wrong and I wasn't ready. Fortunately I was invited by an older friend, Ken Rundell, to work with him at the MRA centre in London, and I accepted with delight. I joined the household at a large house in Charles Street and for the first fortnight was trained to print on a lithograph machine on which we produced each day's news of the work of MRA around the world. This was one of several houses in the area which made up the centre from which we worked.

After supper we men washed up the kitchen utensils – including the large, greasy pots, heavy and hard to clean. When there was a meal for guests, we would often help prepare the vegetables, and there would also be a big wash-up. This would take till near midnight. As we always got up at 6 am for an hour's quiet time, and meals were part of our 'training', that meant some days we happily worked for 18 hours and felt privileged to do so.

In that era there were clear demarcations between men's work and women's work, and even having the men helping with the meals and washing up was quite revolutionary. There were a dozen or more attractive girls training at the centre. None wore lipstick and none of us flirted with them. A redhead was the most attractive, and I was desolate when a team-mate privately disclosed that he was sure God intended him to marry her. We were both wrong, but I was slow to learn not to confuse 'what I want' with 'what God wants' – and that what God wants is always better.

After some months MRA was loaned a house in Bentinck Street with both residential and office accommodation. I lived there for the rest of my time in London. Six days a week we all worked a 16-hour day as a team with no bosses and no official rules, without payment,

It Shouldn't Happen to a Methodist Minister

living by faith. We felt we were part of building 'the new society'.

MRA was involved in many challenging situations, and I was fascinated by the people I met. Jack Manning was a member of the Port Workers Committee that brought about two major strikes in the Port of London in two years. His home had been bombed four times during the war and he blamed 'the business class' – 'the money-grabbers' he called them – as the cause of wars. He had been to a meeting in Canning Town Hall to find out what MRA was up to and heard a representative of 'the boss class' – John Nowell, Managing Director of a Runcorn tannery – telling the story of the drastic change in his own life, which led to transformation in the way he treated his workers. 'This is it,' he said to himself and stayed to talk for two hours after the meeting.

A few months later the men on one wharf in the Port of London were told to load more crates of matches in a hoist than they thought safe. A quarrel broke out. A docker hit the foreman. The wharf manager sacked the docker saying

John Nowell

he wouldn't be employed on the docks again. The dockers protested that this was illegal under the Dock Labour Scheme. Several hundred men went on strike and it was set to become a major dispute.

Jack thought he might help resolve this one, though it meant losing a day's pay to do so. His wife backed him. 'I went first to the foreman,' Jack told us, 'and he wouldn't listen. Then to the man who hit him, and he wouldn't listen. Then I went to the wharf manager and told him that the men thought they were both wrong. I said that I thought we could resolve this matter.' The manager thought for a few minutes then said, 'Well I must admit I was wrong to dismiss him.' He reopened negotiations with the Trade Union officials. The case was argued through the proper channels. The ban was lifted, the man was re-employed and the strike ended.

4
Training for the ministry

MRA gave me a good disciplined training in Christian living in an international team. At the end of 12 months I felt I was ready to offer for the ministry. While I went through the year-long Methodist process of candidating, I decided that I needed to get some experience of the life of an ordinary worker. I found a job as a storeman in a large English Electric factory with 12,500 workers in Liverpool. I chose that factory because I had met one of its union leaders, Pat, whose life had been transformed when he went to see an MRA play.

Broken relationships and strikes were an unresolved national problem in those days, and this factory had its fair share of strife. But Pat's marriage had been saved by his decision to be honest with his wife about his wrongdoing, and he'd decided to work with his union members on the same basis. Instead of just working to increase the wages of his members, he now sought a fair solution for everyone, both the workers and the company. Pat was blunt with fellow workers whenever he felt their demands were not justified, yet he was re-elected by his fellow workers as union leader with an increased majority. The management responded to his new approach, and trust grew. Strikes were no longer needed. I became a team with Pat and every lunchtime joined him with my sandwiches.

A physicist in the factory working on laser research was also active in MRA. He invited me to share his accommodation and his landlady was a splendid cook. After a good evening dinner in our digs he would take me to visit dockers in the port of Liverpool – which had not been without its troubles. I met dockers who were applying MRA's approach and resolving dock disputes. This angered the Communists, who wanted to use disputes to increase bitterness and enlist dockers in their bid to overthrow Britain's political system. I learned of the risk these men took if they stood in the way of Communist plans. 'Accidents' were all too frequent, and a crate could easily fall on a man in the hold below.

The Methodist Church validated my calling and I was sent to theological college in Bristol. But I still had a problem, though I didn't see it at the time. I had become 'spiritually conceited'. In my arrogance I saw MRA as the genuine Methodism which the church was deserting. I regarded theology as pointless theory and philosophy a waste of time. I was more interested in learning Russian.

As part of our training we all had to preach one sermon to the whole college which the tutor then discussed with the college. When it was my turn I preached on Jesus' Sermon on the Mount, saying that this amounted to a call for total honesty, purity, unselfishness and love – and this expressed John Wesley's understanding of 'perfect love' in a nutshell. I didn't add 'and this is MRA' but it was obvious.

The sermon was meaningful to some students. One of them came to me privately and said it helped him decide to live a fully Christian life. But the tutor was suspicious of MRA. He declined to discuss my sermon, cancelling the assessment meeting. It took me many years before I began to realise how arrogant I had been. My MRA experience had enabled me to contribute something of value to some of those preparing for Christian ministry, but I undervalued the college training. When I apologised for my attitude at a college reunion a colleague who had lost his faith came to me and said that my readiness to recognise my failure had given him hope. I began to realise the cost to other people of my attitude.

It Shouldn't Happen to a Methodist Minister

We had little time to meet other university students in Bristol, though I did become friends with an Egyptian. Just after his arrival in 1956, Egypt nationalised the Suez Canal. In response the British, French and Israelis made a secret alliance and invaded Egypt, seizing the Canal. This filled my friend with hatred of Britain, and he resolved to return home at once. After receiving an honest English apology his attitude changed. He decided to stay and take a degree, then go back to work for peace and reconciliation between our two countries. The 'Suez crisis' quickly ended when America told the British to get out and the prime minister resigned. Our imperial pretensions collapsed and the empire gradually dissolved. But our attitudes of superiority have taken a lot longer to die.

My college gave an excellent liberal training through a caring staff. I enjoyed studying the text of the Bible, and I was awarded the university Hebrew prize. I resisted joining the course on philosophy only to find I was told, study philosophy or give up the ministry. Thanks to respected German scholars to whom we deferred, I learnt 'the assured results of modern criticism' which presented the Gospels not as histories but as 'faith' books. It was not possible to find the historical Jesus through the Gospels, they argued, but that didn't matter as all we needed was 'faith'.

It was only later that English scholars saw that the Germans were writing from a different philosophical mindset. The Gospels are now recognised as historical accounts written in a form appropriate to the period – and not as we would write today.

After my three years training I volunteered for missionary work – 'called', I now see, by the glamour of working in Nigeria, which was in the forefront of the news at that time. But I had to go where the missionary society chose and I found I was to be sent to a remote part of Sierra Leone. Since I'd committed myself I was trapped. I was sent to Selly Oak missionary training college for training to prepare me for the work there. I began learning the local language, Mende, studying education since I was to be responsible for 100 schools, how to maintain a land-rover, and other matters needed for life in Sierra Leone at that time.

Halfway through the training a friend from Birmingham called to see me. As a doctor he'd been with the army during the war at the very place I was assigned to. I explained the great work I was going to do, and he listened to me respectfully without saying a word. Then he said to me quite bluntly and simply in the most matter of fact manner: 'If you go to Africa, Africa will be worse after you've gone than before you went.'

I realised at once that he was right. My understanding of Africa and African countries was totally unreal. St Paul says, 'Have a sane estimate of your own capability'. I was naïve about life in a subequatorial country and wholly unsuited for it. I wouldn't even have a picnic in the garden in England because it would attract flies!

I told the missionary secretary that I was no longer sure about my 'call'. He was understanding and released me to be appointed to a circuit at home. As the church had nowhere to send me I was generously kept on at the college for the year, learning Arabic and studying the Holy Koran and Islam with Dr Sweetman. This has since proved helpful in understanding and building relationships with Muslims in this country.

My grandparents had told me of the death of a great Christian, General Gordon, in the Sudan at the hands of 'barbaric natives'. During the year I met students from the Sudan who told me how, in revenge for annihilating Gordon's army, the British sent an army under General Kitchener which defeated the Sudanese and then massacred many Sudanese. One student told me that his grandparents had been tied together and thrown into the Nile.

As a teenager I had been elated to learn of Kitchener's victory and the punishment he administered. I thought this would teach these weird savages, 'whirling dervishes', the lesson they needed. I felt doubly sick when the Sudanese students told me their story. I hope my honest apology for my racist arrogance helped heal their pain a little.

5
Winning the Communists

At the end of my year's training at missionary college I was posted to take charge of eight country churches on the banks of the Humber which included the villages of North Cave and South Cave. I was supposedly a 'probationer' though my Superintendent was nearly 20 miles away and I had to carry out all the duties of a fully ordained Methodist minister.

My largest church was in Brough and as I was a probationer there was no manse. I lived the first fortnight in a caravan belonging to the man who designed the Beverley transporter plane. After that I had a landlady. One night I was awakened by a mouse scratching in my hair, which she found highly amusing.

A secret aeroplane was being developed for the Royal Navy in Brough. A number of my congregation held responsible jobs there and Alf, my leading layman, was the Chief Cashier. He was an excellent steward and had a friendly bulldog. One day the dog was snoring happily and Alf got on the floor, nose to nose, to play with it and said 'woof!' The startled dog woke and bit the first thing it saw. Alf had the embarrassment of explaining to everyone he met what had happened to his nose.

Another member who worked there was Doug who, I was reliably informed, believed the world was flat. Doug was a brilliant mathematician and was said to be able to prove mathematically that planes flying round the earth were in fact flying over it. A Christian fellowship in the factory met at lunchtime every day but told me they spent all their time arguing with Doug. Fortunately it never came up in my conversations with him, and I never knew if he was arguing just for a lark.

My grandfather Coombs had died in 1951, and when Harriet Coombs died in 1958 they left their possessions to a niece, my father and me. This enabled me to buy a car, which I greatly needed to serve the eight churches. My parents were able to buy a house in Rhos-on-Sea where, with my sister, they had a comfortable retirement for 32 years. My sister was able to go on working, and my father to go on preaching till he was 99.

After the Second World War British Communists had little hope of gaining power through the ballot box. So they tried, often successfully, to get control of the docks as a step to wider power. Casual employment meant that a docker never knew when he would get work, and bribing the foreman was the only means of ensuring a job that day. The injustice of this system meant that the Communists were a powerful force in the dockers' unions. The invariable response of the Communists to a dispute was to stop work.

In the Hull docks they called a strike which shut the port down. Everyone was immediately affected as the price of certain foodstuffs in the area rocketed. Joe Hodgson, an MRA full-time worker, had befriended London dockers during the Beaverbrae strike after the war. He used language that the dockers understood: 'change', 'revolution', 'a new world'. When the strike in Hull started, he contacted me and offered to come over and see if he could help. Could I arrange accommodation for him?

I asked Doug who, with his wife, readily agreed to put him up, and Joe came across from Liverpool where he had been working with a dockers' leader named Ernie. Ernie had given him the name and address of the chairman of the trade union leading the Hull strike, and Joe knocked at his door. It was opened by his tigress-like wife Lily – who was used to dealing with newspaper reporters gathered outside. Before the door slammed shut Joe managed to blurt out, 'I've come from Ernie in Liverpool', at which he was dragged inside. She took him straight into the living room at the back where the strike committee was meeting round the table, and gave him an armchair in the corner and a pint mug of tea.

Joe listened to the strike plans until the meeting finished and the members left, leaving just Chairman George. 'Joe's come from Ernie in Liverpool,' Lily said, bringing them each another pint mug of tea, and so at 10 pm their discussion began. It was adjourned at 3 am on condition that Joe would come back the next day and continue it. George had caught on to the fact that Joe was offering him a revolution greater than the one George was involved in, and he was fascinated.

It didn't take George long to decide that Joe's idea of revolution was the one which both he, his members in the union, and the world needed. He soon saw that the current strike issue was bogus, whipped up for Marxist interests that were not those of the dockers, and could be resolved without further strikes. But when his change of view became clear to the strike committee they simply excluded him from the committee.

After a few days Joe had to return to Liverpool, and I was left to do anything I could to help George's growing conviction that cooperation on the docks would be more effective than confrontation. George lived by the docks so he slipped home for lunch every day, and the family invited me to join them. Each day I would nip in with my sandwiches and, over a pint mug of tea, George gave the latest news of his struggle in the port. Having decided that the strike was against his members' interests, he set out to end it. This was tricky as the strike gang surrounded the platform at the weekly mass meetings and he couldn't get near it. This was one of the dodges Communists and their fellow-travellers used to keep control.

At the next mass meeting George started shouting that he wished to speak. Others took up the call, and pushed him forward onto the platform. The strike gang were powerless to stop this. When George spoke, most of the meeting responded warmly to the points he made, and a large majority resolved to end the strike.

The following week the strike was called again, the committee saying they'd found some point that made it necessary. But after a week or two, George managed to finish it for good – and had to endure no little persecution. He was called a 'sky-pilot', a term of derision for Christians supposedly only interested in a 'heaven' in the sky. But a new spirit had started to spread through the docks.

This all gave me material to use in my sermons. I was keen to show that Christianity today was practical in the whole of life, and my congregation appreciated that. After I was ordained by Lord Soper on behalf of the 1960 Methodist Conference, I was asked by the Chairman (Bishop) to stay on in the circuit for a further 12 months, which I gladly agreed to do. As an unmarried minister I soon found that my work was so varied that I never needed a holiday. The periods regarded as officially 'holiday' provided the chance to join in international conferences, theological conferences and retreats. A number of times I attended the annual MRA conferences at Caux, Switzerland.

This conference centre had been bought after the Second World War by 100 Swiss families as a place to help rebuild a shattered Europe. Thousands of French and Germans came together there in the late 1940s, and it has since become a global centre for reconciliation. Many from situations of tensions and conflict have found hope and a new approach there. I would return from my 'holiday' full of new experiences, and with new ideas on how to help people see the relevance of the Christian gospel to their life and work.

6
Theatrical ventures

In 1961 I was invited to Stoke-on-Trent where I had a manse for the first time. I was fortunate to find two elderly maiden sisters who looked after me and the manse while I looked after three churches. One church was alongside a new miners' estate, built for miners from other parts of the country. The church's only nominal contact was the wife of one miner in that street and I went to see her. I had seen a film at Caux, *An idea takes wings*, about the resolution of a fierce industrial conflict in the USA through the change of heart of one of the protagonists. I thought it would interest people in Stoke, which had its own industrial conflict. I offered to show the film in her home. She agreed to invite miners and their wives in the street whom she knew. In the event, only the wives turned up.

They watched the film quietly until the scene where an angry husband cleared the table by drawing together the four corners of the tablecloth and hurling the lot into the kitchen with a great crash. The audience exploded in laughter of recognition. I found out that just before the film one woman had told them all that something similar had happened in her home that very morning. Soon I had got to know families up and down the street.

At the time, MRA was presenting plays at the Westminster Theatre in London's West End. When I arranged a coach for a weekend in London to see a play at the Theatre, it was quickly booked out by couples from the street and their friends. I cannot remember which play they saw, but at the heart of the plays at the Westminster Theatre was the idea that a change of heart can open up entirely new possibilities. Overnight the group were welcomed into the homes of MRA volunteers in London and on the Sunday morning they were invited to a meeting to hear from people who were living the ideas presented in the play, and resolving problems in their families, their colleges, their industries.

During the weeks that followed I visited those who were in the coach party. I listened to a series of extraordinary stories. In a pit where a strike had been threatening, one miner, who had been Mayor of a Lancashire town before he moved to Stoke, told me that after the weekend in London he had gone to the management and union with a new approach, which enabled the dispute to be resolved amicably. His wife had a bitter hatred of the Germans after

The Westminster Theatre

painful war experiences. She told me that she had lost this hatred.

When I knocked on the door of one couple, the wife opened it and burst into tears. 'My husband hasn't beaten me all week!' she said, pulling me inside to see her husband putting up wallpaper for the first time. In the following days I learned that three couples who had talked of divorce were now saying that they thought they could resolve their differences. Another man with a reputation as 'the most foulmouthed in North Staffs' had stopped swearing, and his neighbours asked me what had happened to him. And a 17-year-old came to me and asked for baptism.

Under the rules of the Methodist Church I had been invited to Stoke for three years and a circuit meeting was coming up which could extend my stay for a further two years. All the circuit officials were keen for me to stay and I was willing to do so. But the most influential man in one of my churches decided to get rid of me, and told the Superintendent minister I must go. Only a small number of votes against my staying would end my stay. Everyone heard about it and were expecting an explosive meeting, but the man failed to turn up to the meeting, and my extension of stay was carried unanimously.

I do not know why he objected to me but he may have disliked my emphasis on Christ's standard of honesty. He never said as much to me. In fact I had a cordial relationship with him throughout my tenure in the circuit. But some time later I met someone who as a boy had been in the man's Sunday school class. He told me that after the Sunday school the man would take the class to steal his competitor's cement. I wondered if his conscience was telling him something he couldn't face.

Whatever the reason, I now had a further two years in Stoke, and continued to take parties to the Westminster Theatre. The Theatre had come up for sale soon after

Leslie Marsh

the war. At that time MRA was making much use of theatre to express their ideas, and they decided to buy the Westminster as a memorial to the MRA men and women who had died in war service. Demobbed soldiers gave their gratuities, others contributed, and the theatre was bought. Their aim was to perform plays that were great entertainment and which gave people the opportunity to discover the faith and hope on which all could build a better future.

The first such play, *The Forgotten Factor*, by Alan Thornhill, was described by American President Truman as 'the greatest play to come out of the war'. Based on actual events, it told the story, with much humour and insight, of how a bitter industrial dispute was resolved as the managing director and the trade union leader both began to resolve the conflicts in their own families. Everyone could relate to these conflicts, and audiences loved the play. It ran through the worst winter of the century (and I still shiver today as I remember how cold I was that winter). Yet just as miners came to see it from Stoke, coachloads of miners travelled to London from many other places.

Miners and their families watching 'The Forgotten Factor', North Wales coalfields

It Shouldn't Happen to a Methodist Minister

Scene from 'The Forgotten Factor'

As some of the national media noted, in the mines from which parties had gone to the play, disputes went down and production went up at a time when the country was desperate for coal.

After its London run it toured the country, and in my vacations I helped with the tour. Seeing the play had been an experience of new life for me, as for countless others. I remember in Bristol watching a group of cynical university students who wandered in to take a look and stood at the back. Immediately they were completely captivated.

The Forgotten Factor was followed by a musical, *The Good Road*, and that by another musical, *Jotham Valley* – based on the true story of two brothers who had fallen out and refused to speak, but who found a healed relationship. Then Peter Howard wrote *The Vanishing Island,* a musical which aimed to transform a world of 'getting' into one of 'giving'. It toured across the world by invitation of governments and was credited with helping to begin healing relations between Japan and the Philippines after the terrible suffering inflicted in the war. Howard also wrote a wonderful pantomime, *Give a Dog a Bone*, which filled the theatre every Christmas for many years.

In Stoke-on-Trent Roy, a circuit youth leader, suggested we should put on a play by Peter Howard which he had seen at the Westminster Theatre. *The Ladder* showed the choice between selfish ambition 'going up the ladder' or going towards the cross of Christ: crossing out our selfishness and living a life of service. He offered to direct it with the circuit youth as the cast, and I was asked to take on the project. After its initial performance, churches across the district were bidding to have it, and it was deemed the best event in the district that year.

Then, as Christmas was coming, I wrote *A Farmyard Pantomime*. I had only seen one pantomime in my life. I was three at the time, and ran out of the theatre in fright when the crocodile came on. This didn't deter me, nor did the fact that I'd never written anything. It had little of a plot and the music was simply popular children's songs of the day but it was enjoyed by all.

'Give a Dog a Bone' at Westminster Theatre

It Shouldn't Happen to a Methodist Minister

In the 1960s, some church leaders felt they were leading the world in a new Reformation, based on a morality which replaced negative moral commandments with positive ones. They argued that love is all you need – but, as with the Beatles song, 'All you need is love', love and sex may have sometimes been mixed up. Bishop John Robinson, a leader of the 'new Reformation', described D H Lawrence's novel *Lady Chatterley's Lover* as 'a very moral book'. In my view the Bishop seemed to forget that God's commandments are summed up in 'love your neighbour as you love yourself', and that love is very different to the 'love' which drives the book's protagonists.

I expressed my view in the *Farmyard Pantomime*, but when performance night arrived the leading lady failed to turn up and I was the only person available. I had never acted since my one and only un-performance aged 12, and I was certainly not a singer. But the show had to go on.

Among the characters in the show was a pig reading *Lady Chatterley's Lover* who described himself as a bishop. The *Daily Express*, the largest national newspaper at that time, heard about it and sent a reporter. This led to a centre spread of two pages in the newspaper, which my superintendent minister read to me with delight:

> 'There is no particular significance in the bishop being played by a pig,' Mr Marsh said. 'Any other animal would do …'

I heard from members of my congregation that news of the pantomime also featured on ITV.

Theatre is a hungry animal and another pantomime was needed for the following Christmas. In my congregation was a bass singer with a superb voice, who was ready to perform. This gave me the idea of writing a pantomime with Afro-American spirituals for music. We booked the

Mitchell Memorial Theatre in the centre of the city, and a local amateur theatre enthusiast trained me in theatre production. It didn't have much plot and I relied on the power of the spirituals to carry the audience along.

But as the night for the opening performance approached, the bass singer's firm sent him to France. We found a substitute, but he had dental problems and the dentist removed all his teeth. We went through six basses until in desperation our original bass offered to record all the music, and I had to perform the part, miming the spirituals. In spite of this it was well received and deemed a great success.

Children watching 'Give a Dog a Bone'

7
Britain's first theatre-church

From Stoke I accepted an invitation to a large Victorian church in Bolton, the Seymour Road Wesleyan Chapel, seating around 1,000. There was a plan in place to pull the church down, and replace it with a small dual-purpose building. One morning in my quiet time, a year before we moved to Bolton, the thought came to me that the building could be used as a Christian theatre for the region. I sent the thought to my predecessor who replied explaining that this was impossible 'for the following 12 reasons' – each one convincing. But, he added, I would see for myself when I arrived because in the meantime the demolition of the church had been postponed.

Seymour Road Wesleyan Chapel

I moved to Bolton with the thought out of my mind, but after a couple of months the thought came back, 'Pursue the idea'. This was received warmly by the leading layman whose daughter worked in a firm of architects. She offered to draw up plans. In my innocence I agreed. The firm produced beautiful plans preserving the building virtually as it was with no provision for use as a theatre. It was a non-starter even before we heard the cost, which was far beyond anything the church could raise. When I suggested that it wasn't quite what was needed, she said that there would be added costs if the plans were altered. It cost us a thousand pounds in fees to pay off a contract I didn't even know we had.

I knew that the Westminster Theatre had been converted from a church. I felt we could do the same for a manageable cost. I talked to the man responsible for the Theatre and he offered all the advice I needed free of charge. A quantity surveyor in the church also offered his services free, and he had a good builder friend ready to do the work. I drew up a design and gave detailed measurements. The builder's friendly architect provided working drawings at minimal cost, and others contributed from their expertise.

The transformation of the building would cost £18,000 which we then had the job of raising. We had a cricket field which we sold for £8,000. We then amazingly, received a grant of £4,500 from the Rank Trust, and the congregation raised the rest. A neat design by the builder's architect enabled it to be both a church and theatre, convertible from one to the other. Opened in December 1969, it was claimed to be 'the world's first purpose-built theatre-church'.

Almost a year before the opening I had embarked on something rather important. I had gone to Tirley Garth, an MRA retreat centre in Cheshire, for a few days' break after Easter that year. There, a college friend, Alan, asked me whether I was thinking of marriage.

It Shouldn't Happen to a Methodist Minister

Out with the old!

I admitted that I was rather atheistic about the question. I was now 38 and had been badly bruised by two earlier attempts at marriage. At 17 my first girlfriend had jilted me when I explained that I would not be able to get married for 12 years because I was going to be a Methodist minister and the Church forbad marriage before ordination. With school to complete, army service, university, theological college and three years on probation before ordination, she would have had a long wait... After that I decided not to have a girlfriend until, if God wanted me to marry, I was ready.

Alan suggested I consider marriage seriously like any other proposition. This sounded sensible, and the next morning, in my quiet time, I prayed for God's direction. Immediately the name of Barbara Triggs came to me 'out of the blue'.

She had been one of our large team when I was working in London 14 years earlier. At that time her flat London accent so grated on my Northern ear that I'd thought of her as one girl I'd never marry. However I met her again when I happened to be visiting Tirley Garth several years later. The whole Methodist circuit from a neighbouring town had been invited for the afternoon, and I joined her in entertaining a young couple over the meal. I was struck by the gracious and selfless way she served them.

The next day she couldn't start a car for her driving lesson so I started it for her. But as I began to consider her as a possible marriage prospect the pressure of work meant I soon dropped any thought. Then I began to look around for more immediate local prospects. This merely led to disillusionment.

That afternoon I offered to take Alan to a meeting that evening in Colwyn Bay, and as we were getting near the town Alan asked me, 'Did you have any thought about the question I asked you yesterday?' This put me in a quandary. I had to be honest, but if I said, 'Barbara Triggs,' he might

Barbara Triggs celebrating her birthday

say, 'Oh, you mean Mrs so-and-so'. I concentrated on driving till I hoped he'd forgotten about his question. Then I said, 'I wonder what happened to Barbara Triggs'.

'Oh that's interesting,' Alan said, taking it as the answer to his question. 'She's arranged this meeting, and she's sure to be there.' I was poleaxed. As I drew up to the hotel where the meeting was to take place she was standing on the pavement waiting to greet everybody. I was petrified and didn't look in her direction the whole evening. I managed to drive back to Tirley and a day or two later returned to Bolton.

Three months later I returned to Tirley for my summer holiday. Soon after I arrived, a request was announced for someone to go the next day to Abersoch to project an MRA film for holiday makers. Abersoch was a fashionable resort at the time for Lancashire people with money. There was yachting and pleasant beaches, and a number of them had bought second homes there. The request had come from Barbara Triggs.

I was skilled in projection. The Methodist Home Mission Department had given me responsibility for distributing projectors to Methodist churches through the North West of England and Wales. So I was an obvious candidate. Once a week for three weeks I went with Alan to Abersoch. We projected the film in the evening, were given hospitality by locals overnight, enjoyed the resort the next morning, and had lunch with Barbara and Margaret Burton, a medical doctor with whom she lived.

By the third week my mind was made up. After lunch Alan and Margaret quietly withdrew to the front room and I was left to help Barbara wash the dishes. She had not given me much attention, but being sociable she asked, 'What would you like to do this afternoon?' I began clumsily to tell her that I was thinking about marriage. She interrupted, pointing out that it was not appropriate to talk with her about such a personal matter. This strengthened my determination, and I went straight ahead and proposed. She rapidly left the room.

Forty-eight anxious hours later the phone rang. To my great joy, she accepted my proposal. I had said to her that Jesus would always come first in my life, and this, she said later, gave her the courage to accept.

Soon I was back in Abersoch, and we were getting to know each other. I discovered she was an artist who had raised thousands of pounds for charity, winning many commissions. She currently had an exhibition of her paintings in Abersoch, and took me to see it.

This began my appreciation of painting. At the age of ten I had been turned out of my school art class after my one and only lesson. The teacher had told us all to paint a galleon. Five were selected for display on the classroom wall – four as examples of how to do it and one how not to. The following week I was put in the weaver's class to make a scarf.

Our wedding

8
Better than a thousand sermons

We honeymooned in Machynlleth, where Barbara painted and I worked on a musical about St Joan of Arc for our new theatre-church. The hotel cleaning ladies were much amused that Barbara put up all our wedding cards in our hotel room. Apparently most newly-weds attempt to conceal the fact. I hadn't noticed that she had put them up. She told me I was not observant and took me in hand.

She taught me a lot, and I am grateful to have been able to appreciate art ever since. Barbara continued to paint throughout our marriage. I helped her mount exhibitions in all kinds of settings, from a fashionable department store to a school hall. All the money she raised went to charity.

Life with me was not easy for her. The work of the theatre-church was heavy. I had to get up very early, on occasion at 4 am, and only got home again at 10 pm. Some may be built for such a life but I wasn't. I remember feeling at the end of one rehearsal that I was passing out. Fortunately the theatre was only fifty yards from our house and I managed to stagger home and collapse into bed.

Until then I had done little housework. While I lived in Stoke the Nowell sisters looked after me, and they had moved with me to Bolton. Before them the church had arranged for a lady to come in to cook and clean. When I'd started at Cambridge we were all given a thorough medical. The consultant punched me in the stomach and said 'Did that hurt?' When I said 'Yes' he gave me an instruction paper saying I must have 20 minutes rest after every meal and not drink alcohol. I followed both injunctions.

This was a shock to Barbara. She told me later that she cried when she realised that I expected her to do the cooking, washing up and housework. I am ashamed of my insensitivity. But I don't remember her ever nagging me. Our situation changed over the years. When the children were very young and I was running the theatre-church, we invited Dagny, the daughter of a Norwegian concert pianist, who wanted to come to England as a nanny and polish her English. She was a real help for Barbara – and also in writing out music for the shows. Later, as the children were growing up I took a lot of responsibility for them, and after I retired from pastoral responsibility I was able to help more with the housework. But cooking has always remained an art beyond me.

We arrived home from our honeymoon to help transform our church into a theatre-church, equipped with

Bolton theatre church

It Shouldn't Happen to a Methodist Minister

Both church and theatre

the latest technology of a West End stage. This technology was also used in worship, and the congregation responded enthusiastically. But I had to complete *St Joan*, both script and music, and gather a cast of actors and singers for an opening night in November 1969. I was a novice at writing music. I'd been taught the piano to about grade five and could play hymn tunes, but I'd done no music theory. There was a girl in the congregation whom I hoped would play the part of Joan. She had some music training and, with her help, a score was produced. The songs would not perhaps have satisfied a professional composer, but in Bolton they were being sung like pop songs months afterwards.

Among her accomplishments, Barbara had been a costume designer and costume maker for West End shows in London. That solved a problem I hadn't even thought of. Artists and carpenters volunteered to create the stage sets, a choreographer and an experienced lighting engineer offered their services. A West End actor came up and polished the production. And so almost miraculously the show was ready and received an excellent review by the local theatre critic and the press. But what moved me most was people's response.

One of my oldest church members told me with deep conviction: 'That play meant more to me than a thousand sermons'. I was thrilled, even if he didn't do much for my ego as a preacher. And one morning a young woman knocked at my door. She told me: 'I have three young children and last night I'd just left the hospital where the doctors had told me there was no hope for my husband. I thought I couldn't go on with my life. But on the way home I went into your theatre. When I came out I had found the courage to face life again.' To me it was worth it just for that one stranger. The fortnight of performances was a sell-out and we wished we could continue, but the cast had full-time jobs and commitments and it was impossible.

Barbara designing costumes

I now had to write and compose a second musical on a similar scale and the idea came to me that I could tell the story of St Francis. Almost miraculously it came together again. A local magician even lent me his dove! Again the show received excellent reviews. 'This is a musical that can hold its own with many a secular professional counterpart and more than equal with several,' wrote the theatre critic of the *Methodist Recorder*. 'The production sang its way into the hearts of the audience from the opening to the finale, "Sing the song of the sun!"'.

I then wrote a play about John Wesley. His work inspired a new dignity and moral authority in many working people, and in the chapels they learned to speak effectively in public. This enabled them to play a significant role in the growth of the trade union movement in Britain. The play concluded with the story of the Tolpuddle martyrs, who many see as the first trade unionists.

I followed this with a musical farce about another Adam and Eve on a new planet in the time of the Cold War, *Fancy meeting you here!* No one was willing to take the part of the devil so I was forced to play it myself. A playwright and actress, Nancy Ruthven, offered to produce it for me, which I accepted with delight, as we now had a young daughter, Jo, and another on the way. People said it had the audience 'rolling in the aisles', and fortunately few noticed that I hadn't managed to work the ending out properly.

The play was so well received that Nancy offered to produce *He was not there*, a Christmas play by actress Phyllis Austin for the festive season. Nancy then joined with composer Kathleen Dodds creating a superb musical out of the Victorian children's classic, *The Princess and the Goblin*.

By then we had two daughters, Jo and Louise. Each year, for summer and winter holidays, we were able to take them

Leslie Marsh

'The Princess and the Goblin', produced by Nancy Ruthven, music by Kathleen Dodds

'The Princess and the Goblin'

to my in-laws who lived by the sea on the south coast at Pagham, and with my parents in North Wales at Rhos-on-Sea.

Barbara, Louise, Joanna at Rhos-on-Sea

9
John Wesley takes to the stage

A former President of the Methodist Church and historian, Dr Maldwyn Edwards, had asked the playwright Alan Thornhill to write a show about John Wesley. Alan protested that he could not do justice to such a wide-ranging life as Wesley's. So Maldwyn gave Alan the story of Martha Thompson, a 17-year-old girl who ran away from home in Preston to London, where she was employed by a quack doctor. One day she heard John Wesley preach and was converted. This infuriated her employer, who put her in Bedlam, the 'madhouse', where most inmates died within 18 months. When John Wesley heard her story he got her out of Bedlam and rode her home to Preston on the back of his own horse.

The Bolton cast who performed 'Ride! Ride!'

Alan Thornhill was a professional playwright, far more able to write a play on Wesley than my earlier amateur attempt. He collaborated with Penelope Thwaites, the Australian concert pianist and composer, and together they incorporated an array of catchy songs with brilliant lyrics. It was titled *Ride! Ride!* The national Methodist Drama Committee, of which I'd been made Secretary, asked me to produce it, and Nancy Ruthven again came to direct. Penelope came as accompanist with one or two local musicians. I am no singer but, against my will, I was persuaded to take the part of John Wesley. My only audition was to see if I could sing loud enough and I managed to pass – just.

The response to *Ride! Ride!* was overwhelming. We were invited to give the show alongside the national Methodist Conference in Newcastle that year. There we had two full houses of 1,100 each in the People's Theatre. Both audiences gave a tumultuous response. Next morning the Conference was astounded when the President began by asking for an emergency resolution. In its hundred-year history this had never happened. The resolution – that *Ride! Ride!* be presented throughout the country – was passed unanimously with great enthusiasm.

That was not possible for an amateur cast. If *Ride! Ride!* was to progress it would have to be a professional production. Besides, I was moving again. As in my first circuit I required an almost unanimous vote in the annual circuit meeting. Though the meeting was overwhelmingly in favour of me continuing, three hostile votes were enough to vote me out.

Some time before, the circuit auditor had come to see me in the middle of lunch one Sunday to tell me that monies for which a church official was responsible were missing. The auditor had found that a number of receipts signed by this official had been forged, and there were other irregularities. I talked to the official but could get no sense out of him. So I had to bring a charge in the Church Council.

The official was highly regarded by Council members, who were outraged at the mere suggestion of dishonesty. I called in the Superintendent minister to handle it. He told me that some time earlier the official had approached him with two others to complain that I preached morality instead of the gospel, and demanded to have me removed.

When the Superintendent presented all the facts, the shocked Church Council agreed to remove the offender swiftly from both office and church membership. How much money the church lost was never known. But the

Leslie as John Wesley in 'Ride! Ride!'

whole episode left a sour taste among some of the church members.

However, I had an interesting position to move on to. Ron, my chairman, had arranged for me to become chaplain at Cardiff University, with charge also of a large church in Cwmbran until the chaplaincy became a full-time job, scheduled for a year later.

John Gibbs, the chairman of the Drama Committee, who lived nearby, decided to bring together a South Wales cast and produce *Ride! Ride!* for the following year's Methodist Conference in Bristol. He asked me to play Wesley again but insisted that my singing be made at least a little more presentable. I was funded for a month's singing lessons at the Welsh National School of music and drama. Again the show was a triumph and boosted hopes of a national production.

Louise and Joanna in 'Ride! Ride!'

10
Challenging apartheid

At the start of 1974 I was invited to an international multi-racial Easter conference in Pretoria hosted by MRA. Apartheid had become an international issue, and Pretoria was known as 'the bastille of apartheid'. I hadn't the money to go but, out of the blue, a church member unexpectedly gave me what, with reduced fares, was just enough for the flight.

At the conference I shared a room with a black headmaster from Soweto, and preached to a large multi-racial congregation in the Central Methodist church in the city. Both MRA and the Methodists were determined to demonstrate that apartheid had no part in a truly Christian South Africa. They offered a model for the future.

For many the present was dire. One young African told me that he and a friend overtook a car which contained two young white men. The car immediately passed them and forced them to stop. The two white men got out and told them 'black men must never overtake white men', and as punishment took his wrist watch and other valuables before letting them go. It was deeply painful to hear such stories.

The conference was organised by South Africans determined to change such attitudes, and they launched it in the magnificent amphitheatre of the University of South Africa, which juts out dramatically from a hillside above the city of Pretoria. A thousand people filled it – black, white and brown, sitting side by side. Among them were senior Afrikaners, ministers of the Dutch Reformed Church, black leaders, prominent men and women from what were

University of South Africa

then known as the Coloured and Indian communities. For Pretoria such a meeting was a first, believed impossible by most locals. But my MRA colleagues were determined to do it and, with much persistence, they succeeded.

The Mayor of Pretoria extended his city's welcome. Then recently retired Supreme Court Justice C J Claassen, set the tone: 'My whole attitude to many other races was completely wrong. There was racial superiority and indifference towards Africans, Asians, Jews and Coloured people. This meant an apology to many individuals and to all. I went to the capital of Basutoland and in the national assembly I apologised to the leaders of that great nation for my wrong personal attitude.'

George Daneel, Minister of the Dutch Reformed Church and former Springbok rugby player, followed up: 'We as whites have an enormous responsibility. Change begins not when we point out the faults of others, but when we face our own. The future depends on whether we can win the trust of men of different races.'

To me the practice of apartheid was ludicrous. There were separate post-offices for black and white and banks had separate counters, but in large stores black and white assistants together served black or white customers. In the Rand Central Building where MRA had an office there were four lifts, three for whites and one for blacks. MRA suggested to all 500 offices in the building that it would be better for everyone to use any lift. All agreed except one office. Three lifts were duly changed to 'for everyone', leaving one for whites only. Blacks going down tended to use the white lift to enjoy being berated half-heartedly by the black janitor as they left the lift at the bottom!

Throughout the conference the question of the country's future was thrashed out with much plain talking, as 350 of the delegates, of all colours, lived together in an hotel in the centre of the city. Professor M E R Mathiva of South Africa's biggest black university, speaking on Good Friday, said, 'We are facing the challenge of the Cross for a black South African like myself, and for white South Africans. Fear is the most important factor in our country. Out of fear comes hatred. Hatred and fear accompany each other like two friends on one path. They bring despair. We need to face our sins against the mothers of all our children, black and white.'

A prominent Afrikaaner spoke of his 'pain and shame for the many people who have suffered as a result of the self-righteousness, arrogance and superiority of so many of my people. My own sin,' he went on, 'has been indifference and lack of concern at the circumstances in which others find themselves.' An African doctor from one of the sprawling urban 'townships' near Pretoria joined them on the platform. 'This is one of the few occasions in my life,' he said, 'when the utterance of a white man has been able to feed emotion not of anger nor of hatred but to return me to

Christ's teaching.' The theme of that meeting was 'An Easter experience valid for East and West'.

I appreciated a breakfast with Richard Brown, the African-American Dean of a university college in the USA which had become mixed race, both students and staff, after Martin Luther King's work led to the desegregation of US education. Most of the white staff accepted an African-American Dean, but three white lecturers were hostile and showed it. One morning in his quiet time he told God, 'I know I should love them. I've done everything I can to love them, but I hate them!' God said to him, 'You can't help how you feel but you can help how you act. Treat those three men as your best friends.' It was tough to do but he did it. Everyone knew the situation and the unspoken reaction on the campus was 'the Dean's gone nuts'. It became a joke.

'After a few days I began to see what a crazy joke it was and it became easier,' he told me. 'After three months I found I was loving them. At the end of the first year one knocked at my door and offered his help with my extra workload. At the end of the second year the second one asked to talk about a personal problem he couldn't talk to anyone else about. Five years later the third too became a best friend.'

* * *

I had been told I would become the full time chaplain at Cardiff University the following year. But while I was in South Africa another minister was invited by the circuit stewards to take this position. This was announced officially at the circuit meeting soon after my return. I was flabbergasted and protested, but it was a done deal. I had to take on another church to complete the standard three years of a minister's tenure, which I was very happy to do. When that concluded, I moved to Cwmbran.

Leslie Marsh

We counted many nationalities among our friends in South Wales

There we had to decide on our daughters' schooling. At the time there was an educational fashion to give the children more say in what and how they were taught. Some cynically described this as 'let the children teach the teachers'. The circuit stewards, both teachers at the Comprehensive School, urged us to send our daughters to a primary school which didn't follow this fashion, and we took their advice.

I found that our six-year-old daughter was a year behind in her reading and the school quickly remedied this. It was a large primary but the Head insisted on hearing every child read, and no child left her school unable to do so. It equally suited our younger daughter when she started. As I picked her up for the last Easter holiday there she burst into tears. 'There isn't any school for a fortnight,' she wept – quite a recommendation for the school, because I don't think that home was all that bad.

Unlike Barbara, I had little understanding of parenting. She was 16 when a baby brother arrived in the family.

She later looked after a baby full-time for a year, and then helped bring up the two children of a couple where the father was ill and mother his full-time carer. So she was able to train me. When 'Stop it!' was my invariable reaction to whatever our elder child was doing, my wife gently led me to decide on three things to which we would say 'No': no fingers in the electric sockets, no licked fingers in the sugar bowl, and no picking up the cat (poor cat…). For the rest I learned to put up with it till later we would be able to add more.

When our younger daughter was four, I happened to glance out of the window where children were playing and saw a boy her age kicking her on her shins. As he heard me open the front door he was off faster than I could run after him. 'Why did you let him do that?' I asked my daughter. 'You must stand up for yourself and give him a good kick back!' Later she said to me, 'I'm not going to be a Christian.' She had been ready not to return wrong for wrong, as her Daddy had taught her. But she found it too much to bear his anger for doing so. It was a lesson for Daddy.

Barbara with Joanna and Louise   *Leslie and Louise*

11
Ride! Ride! goes national

To fulfil the Newcastle Conference resolution to take *Ride! Ride!* through the country we set up a charitable trust to run a professional production. Ron Mann, a Methodist from Wimbledon experienced in theatre production, was made secretary and he and John Gibbs were largely responsible for raising the £30,000 needed for this task. Ron agreed to be producer. He appointed one of the best-known directors of musicals, Peter Coe, and booked eleven of the largest theatres in the country in all the main cities.

This was an enormous financial commitment for us and a colossal risk. We had no money to cover it and we took the decision in faith, believing that audiences everywhere would pay theatre prices to come and see it. Ron visited all the Methodist Chairmen (our equivalent of bishops) who each gave a capable man in their district the task of promoting it.

Ron Mann, Secretary, Aldersgate Productions

The tour was a virtual sell-out everywhere. *The Guardian* called it 'one of the most astonishing theatrical events we are likely to see this year'.

It had its amusing moments. The play began with John Wesley addressing the audience directly. 'Let me ask you in tender love, is your city a Christian city? Are you living portraits of Jesus Christ? Are your magistrates honest and all your heads of government all of one heart and soul?' In

It Shouldn't Happen to a Methodist Minister

Scene from 'Ride! Ride!' – painting by Barbara Marsh

Newcastle at the time, the city council had been cheated of a large sum of money, and a great laugh went up when one of the audience called out, 'By golly, they are not'!

And it made a profound impression. One minister wrote to the *Methodist Recorder* saying it had 'renewed his whole ministry'. A number of men were inspired to offer themselves for the ministry. (At that time ministry was confined to men.) After the national tour it ran for

76 performances in the West End of London. In total, over 100,000 people saw it. It has since been performed extensively in the United States, and in several other countries.

The members of the cast were typical professional actors. I joined them at the week's showings in Hull and enjoyed one actor's response to a cynical radio interviewer who asked if the play had 'changed' him yet. In fact he'd been facing up to Wesley's plain honesty when he read the play and it had necessitated some considerable financial restitution. 'I can't say,' he replied, 'but my creditors seem very pleased.' He was not the only one to find themselves 'changed' by John Wesley. The lead actor playing the part of John Wesley, Gordon Gostelow, had been known in the profession as difficult to work with. After the run of *Ride! Ride!* people remarked on the change in his approach. When he died, *The Guardian* carried an obituary which included this paragraph:

> After a nationwide tour *Ride! Ride!* ran for three months at the Westminster Theatre. Having been cast just five days before rehearsals started, with no prior knowledge of the subject, Gostelow spent the run 'trying to understand the man'. Asserting that 'the theatre has always failed religion', he was also convinced that 'You have got to honour what [Wesley] was on about. As an actor, all the time you're trying to get to the guts of the thing.'

When *Ride! Ride!* closed after its three-month run in the West End, we were unanimous that we should continue with this work, and become an ecumenical body. The Archbishop of Canterbury and the Cardinal Archbishop of Westminster each appointed a director and over the next 10 years as a charitable company, Aldersgate Productions, we launched 20 shows into the West End.

One Christmas we launched the first theatrical production of C S Lewis's book, *The Lion, the Witch and the Wardrobe*. This proved to be the most successful family show in the West End that season. The *Daily Mail* described it as a 'gloriously thrill-packed fantasy'. It followed this with a tour to 26 British cities. We went on to perform productions of two of C S Lewis's subsequent books, *The Voyage of the Dawntreader* and *The Magician's Nephew*. And we produced *Song of the Lion*, C S Lewis's own story as told in his book, *Surprised by Joy*.

Other shows included a play by Karol Wojtyła, who became Pope John Paul II. Another, written by Václav Havel, first President of the Czech Republic, had been credited with helping to end the Communist dictatorship in the country. Journalist Malcolm Muggeridge and Alan Thornhill collaborated on a play *Sentenced to Life*, dealing with the plight of a paralysed woman who asks her husband to kill her. The play, which argues against euthanasia, challenged a pro-euthanasia play *Whose Life is it Anyway?* at the Mermaid Theatre. *The Financial Times* wrote: 'They are fighting out the controversy of euthanasia at two theatres, one at each end of London.' BBC One's *Tonight* programme featured a discussion with clips from *Sentenced to Life*. Ned Chaillet in *The Times* wrote, 'It is good to see that the theatre can still play a role in great moral controversies.'

We also contacted two small education theatre companies which were performing plays in London schools, and invited them to perform for a couple of weeks at the Westminster Theatre. This raised their profile and we cooperated well.

But by the 1990s the costs had become prohibitive, and our two star producers Ron Mann and John Gibbs had died through cancer. Sadly, as Secretary, I was left to close the charity.

Leslie Marsh

The legacy of Aldersgate lives on in plays performed and films produced in many countries. As Nigel Goodwin, a Board Member of Aldersgate, said: 'Our commitment to the highest professional standards was vital. So often you see something in a church basement which is so poor. People say it is good enough for God, but it is not. One of Aldersgate's by-products was to set a standard for what Christian theatre can be.

'Our plays are not a preaching vehicle in one sense,' he went on. 'They raise questions so that people can come to their own conclusions. They show both the rainbows in life and the thunderstorms which produce them. The church often only wants the rainbows.'

Poster for 'Ride! Ride!'

12
Mental illness

While we were in Cwmbran we were hit one morning out of the blue by something I had almost forgotten. Before I married Barbara, Margaret Burton, the medical doctor with whom she was living, called me aside to explain Barbara's medical condition. Margaret told me that Barbara was termed manic/depressive (now bi-polar), and at one stage she had been so affected that she had been placed in the padded cell of an Oxford hospital.

At the time she was living with a family active in MRA's work. The husband had had a heart attack and Barbara joined them to help care for their two young children. When Barbara came out of hospital in Oxford she had gone to North Wales to help Margaret care for her two elderly parents in a situation where there were not the same pressures and she could fully recover. She had recovered, but Margaret warned me that if she should become ill again I would need to call for medical help immediately.

Margaret did not question the wisdom of our getting married. But I was left with the question, was I ready to marry someone who could become mentally incapacitated, and love and care for her for the rest of her life? After careful thought I made the decision that I was.

One morning in Cwmbran Barbara didn't get up. I assumed she had a common illness and asked if she'd like breakfast in bed. She replied 'a carrot'. I got one and she then teased me by pretending to eat it, so I went downstairs to my desk in our living-room/office hoping she'd soon feel better.

Leslie Marsh

The Conwy Valley, Wales, looking towards Snowdonia – a painting by Barbara Marsh

Halfway through the morning I suddenly heard her coming thumping down the stairs. Fortunately the door onto both the bottom of the stairs and front door was by my desk and I opened it as she reached the bottom step. She was dressed simply in her nightie and she reached out and grabbed the front door handle and started to open it as I tussled to stop her. 'I've got to go up the mountain,' she exclaimed in a strange voice. There was a mountain behind our house and we had recently seen Peter Howard's play *Mr Brown comes down the hill*, in which Christ returns on a mountain today. Fortunately I won the tussle.

Barbara had been perfectly well and given birth to our two daughters during the first ten years of our marriage and I had almost forgotten about the bi-polar. I now realised what was happening. After I got her back to bed I rang the doctor, who called the consultant. The consultant came immediately and arranged an ambulance to take Barbara into hospital. I visited her that night and found she was refusing to take any medication. She didn't recognise me and denied that I was her husband.

When word went round about her absence the ladies in all the churches formed a rota to provide meals for me and the children, and I well remember how good those meals were. The girls were philosophical. At one breakfast I had to listen to a clinical dissection by a four and a six-year-old as, disregarding my presence, they discussed whether it was better to have Daddy or Mummy ill.

The consultant said Barbara would recover, but it would take six months. She advised electrical brain treatment, electro-convulsive therapy for which I would need to sign my approval. I'd seen an article in *The Guardian* which was negative about this treatment so I was worried. I rang a consultant friend in Birmingham. After talking with his colleague he rang back the next day to say 'It works like a dream'. I signed the form.

The evening after the treatment I found her tired but restored to her senses. The next morning, after a second treatment, I found her fully restored, and she joked about being in 'the looney bin'. They kept her for a day or two for observation, then she returned home from hospital as fit as ever.

After that Barbara began to recognise the moment she felt an episode was starting, and took action to avoid it developing. I also realised that the evening before her collapse something was not quite right about the cheese on toast she served for supper. This gave me a clue on how to pick up any unusual behaviour and help reduce any pressure she might feel. In this way Barbara was able to avoid any serious episode for the next 35 years.

13
An unlikely setting for musical prowess

I was due to stay in Cwmbran, a 'Home Mission' appointment, for five years and my Chairman had reassured me that no way would I have to move any earlier. Then at the end of the fourth year I suddenly discovered in a casual conversation with a member of the District Committee that Home Missions no longer had the money to finance the appointment and I would have to move on. 'Hasn't anybody told you?' asked my informant, aghast.

It was a blow. I had been talking with members in the London area about a move there the following year where we could create another theatre-style church and try out Christian plays with unemployed actors at very little cost, reducing the risk of losing a lot of money on a full West End production. Now all such ideas were in ruins. I became bitter at the way I had been treated. For two months I nursed my bitterness till one morning God opened my eyes and I saw that I must let it go. This happened, and that was a 'miracle'. But such 'miracles', I found, tend to lead to more 'miracles'.

The only appointment left was the circuit next to my father's last circuit in the West Midlands, where no minister had been willing to go. I was soon to find out why. The manse needed a new heating system, carpeting, kitchen floor covering, decorating throughout, everything. The new circuit stewards were determined to bring it up to standard, but they couldn't do it overnight. We had to leave all our

Cradley, West Midlands, was part of my circuit – painting by Barbara Marsh

furniture, the cat and everything behind in the manse in Cwmbran, and camp in our new manse until it was ready for all our belongings.

We arrived, each of us equipped with a camp bed, mug, spoon, knife and fork and moved from room to room as the workmen required. One day my clerical collar was swept up and disappeared with the decorator's rubbish so for my induction service the congregation weren't quite sure whether they were getting a minister or layman.

Sadly the former circuit steward's wife died just after I arrived. Her husband had then moved in with his son-in-law and family where I went to see them. I quickly realised that he had made all the funeral arrangements and my part was simply to walk in the funeral procession with three former ministers. The funeral was to be taken by a minister who was coming specially for the occasion.

Unfortunately the day chosen was the very day I had to go back to Cwmbran to oversee moving our belongings to our new manse. This date had been arranged with great difficulty and couldn't be changed, so I had to explain that I would have to miss the funeral. This produced a torrent that any sergeant-major would have been proud of, interrupted at last by his exasperated son-in-law shouting, 'Shut up!' 'I will not!' roared his father-in-law. 'You'll shut up or you'll leave this house!' thundered his son-in-law – which finally did the trick and ended the most unusual funeral interview of my ministry.

The ethos of the area was set against education. It had been the world centre of the chain-making industry and life expectancy was below 40, so the workers saw no point in wasting time on education – and from the employers' point of view there was no point in providing it. When a bright teenager won a place at Warwick University her parents did everything they could to 'save' her from it.

Our elder daughter Jo topped her year of 200 children, but I was astonished to discover that they wouldn't even put her in for 'O levels', only the less demanding CSEs. She was already, at age 11, doing music for grade 8 outside school. One of my churches had a good electronic organ so I started her on that. Unfortunately the steward was horrified at a child touching the organ and banned it at once.

So I approached the Anglican vicar, and he was delighted to have her practice on his church organ. Michael

Jonathan Sparey, violinist, training Jo and Louise, Tirley Garth

Haynes from the Birmingham School of Music was organist there, and he tutored her.

Louise, aged eight, had to play the piano for the school assembly and show her teacher how to play the recorder so that he could teach the class. She had so loved school in Cwmbran but after a few weeks in her new school she said to me plaintively, 'Can I leave school now. I've learnt enough to live.' Her teacher was 'mad' – the Head's word – on physical education. One day he kept Louise running round the field until she collapsed and I had to carry her home.

Providentially some charitable trusts made it possible for us to send her to board at Birmingham Blue Coat School where the head was a doctor of music and she became happy again.

But they both needed a more challenging school setting. At that point the Government started the Assisted Places scheme, which enabled both children to go to my old school, Kingswood School, Bath, founded for the children of Methodist ministers. While there, Jo became Choir Director of a Bath church, and Louise became organ scholar at Bath Abbey. Jo then gained a scholarship to Sidney Sussex College Cambridge, and Louise gained a scholarship to Lincoln College Oxford.

Louise at Bluecoat School

14
A cure to corruption

In the 1980s there was terrible unemployment in the West Midlands. Brian, my old college friend, who had married an Australian, brought his wife Lorna to visit us. He had been doing remarkable work in Australia. In Queensland there had been much anger at corruption in government. Brian realised that corruption does not start with $30,000 bribes. It starts through a culture where citizens think some dishonesty, such as cheating on taxes, is acceptable. So he created a pledge form which he offered to those who were unhappy about the government corruption – a pledge to refuse all corruption themselves, to pay their taxes honestly, and to vote for candidates of integrity. Many in his church signed it. Then he went to his Member of Parliament, who signed it too. It featured in the media, and other people took the pledge around. Before long thousands of people had signed it.

Brian Lightowler

What difference this made in Queensland Brian could not estimate. But staying with him was a teacher from Taiwan. At the time, in Taiwan, some parliamentary candidates simply bought their way into Parliament through bribery. They were known as 'golden ox' candidates. The teacher decided to try Brian's approach. There the pledge caught on in a big way. Eventually 700,000 people signed it, including many politicians. When the election took place, many of the 'golden ox' candidates were voted out. The campaign continued through the following elections, and is recognised as having brought major change. The organisation measuring electoral integrity now rates Taiwan eighth best in the world.

One evening I invited in a young man to meet Brian and Lorna. Brian told of his decision to take time in quiet, seeking God's direction, and some of the outcomes from that decision. My young friend was fascinated. He decided to do the same the next morning. The first thought that came to him was, 'Take the proper time for your tea-break'. He knew at once what it meant.

He worked for a canal boat builder, and they only had one order on their books. So they slowed down their work on this order, extending the morning tea break to keep the work going as long as possible. At the next tea break, as soon as the allotted time was up, my friend got up, took his mug and washed it. His mates were not pleased. But one by one they began to copy him. My friend decided to do his best on the job and, again, others followed him. It wasn't long before the boat was finished. The customer was so delighted to get the boat on time and of such good quality that he ordered another boat on the spot.

One week a woman appeared in the back pew of one of my churches. She left quickly at the end of the service before anyone had a chance to speak to her. The same thing happened the following two weeks, so I asked someone next time to catch her and invite her to call in at the manse for coffee. One morning she came.

It turned out that Jill had an unhappy home life, suffered from epilepsy, had three difficult young children, and a husband who was beginning to stray to another woman. Life had become too much. She had sought help from various sources without avail, so had decided to end her life. In the middle of the night she had taken her pills out of the drawer, determined to take the lot.

At that point she wondered if she'd tried everything and she thought of the church. She had never been to a church but her day school teacher had taught them the Lord's prayer. She recited it, then decided the next Sunday to go to the nearest church, and put her pills back in the drawer. Her nearest church happened to be one of mine, and there she says she found peace for the first time in 10 years.

But the moment she got home and touched the door handle there was a great bellow inside, 'Where's my dinner?' and that peace was gone. Yet she felt that she could live another week if only she could find that peace again the following Sunday. This time it lasted a little longer. And longer again the third week after which she'd arrived at the manse.

Barbara talked with her about taking time in quiet. The thought that God had a purpose for her life and that he could speak to her was transformative. She left the manse set on listening for God's will. Soon she was encountering what seemed to her like miracles.

One of their problems was noisy next-door neighbours. When the neighbours made too much noise they hammered on the wall, at which the neighbours hammered back. A contest ensued as to who could hammer hardest. The next time the contest began, she had the thought to go round and apologise for having the TV on too loud. "Won't you come in?" responded her astonished neighbour, who went on to explain to Jill that her marriage was falling apart and that they were on the point of divorce.

Jill passed on to her some of Barbara's suggestions. 'Everybody wants to see the other person change their ways but everybody is waiting for the other person to begin. If you want to see things different the practical place to begin is with yourself.' Her neighbour applied this simple truth and her marriage was saved – and this was just the first of the marriages saved by Jill.

Jill was convincing because she lived the way she talked about. Her husband Mel watched this approvingly. He'd never had anything to do with church but began to make one or two necessary changes himself. Having a 'new' wife, the other lady disappeared from his mind.

Mel worked for Bulldog Clips, where he was classed as neither management nor worker, so he hadn't concerned himself with disputes at the factory. Now he started to get involved. One dispute became so intense that it threatened to close the factory, and Mel realised that he was friends with people active on both sides of the dispute. These friendships enabled him to be the catalyst who brought the two sides together, enabling them to find a solution and save the factory for a few more years.

At home where there had been rows, now there was a way to resolve them. The three children still remember the transformation. Jill took a job as a lollipop lady, helping children cross the road at the primary school. There she got to know the families in that part of town. Soon her home became a place where people came with their family or other problems.

One Friday evening Jill answered the door to find their other next-door neighbours asking to talk. The husband explained that he was working for a company in Birmingham which, that afternoon, had suddenly announced to the workers – as they were given their week's pay – that they were all redundant. The firm was being taken over that weekend by another firm. The neighbour himself had been there all his working life. What could he do about it?

Mel and Jill told them of taking time in quiet to listen for the thoughts that came, and what this had done for them. A few days later they told Jill what happened when they tried. The husband realised that he'd left his desk in a mess and that he could go in on Monday morning and offer to tidy it up. This he did. The new manager said that he was looking for someone in that department – would he like the job? He was given his job back on the spot. I never discovered whether others had the same experience.

During my time in Cwmbran I had read *A historian's reading of the Gospels* by the great Jewish British scholar Geza Vermes. It convinced me that a historical study of Jesus was possible, and in my last months in Cwmbran I started a Bible reading group with this aim. When I moved to the West Midlands I found that the local Queen's College library had a small section labelled 'Historical Jesus', and I was given access. Earlier quests for a historical Jesus having failed, what is now called the 'third quest' was just beginning. New historical methods and tools had been developed, a new international quest was underway, and scholars from very different backgrounds and points of view were now researching with the aim of uncovering the real Jesus.

The Bible reading course in Cwmbran was much appreciated. So when I'd moved to the West Midlands in 1980 I decided to continue with a weekly 'class' on the historical Jesus. One day I visited a young couple who'd just moved into the area. I discovered that they had been Methodists but neither of them were now interested in attending church. However, when I mentioned a historical study of Jesus that appealed to the wife.

She came to the class for the first three weeks. The following week husband Peter appeared instead. Peter had been so interested in what his wife had told him that he claimed a turn to come, leaving his wife to look after their baby. Peter spent a happy evening arguing against everything I said, and came to do the same again the following week – but this time a little less strongly. And so it went on each week, Peter becoming less argumentative and more interested in Jesus.

Peter worked in social services, and his aim was to become the head of social services for the region. When one evening two MRA friends from Coventry, Patrick and Margaret O'Kane, visited me I suggested they drop in on Peter and his wife. They spent the evening with them and when it got late Patrick said, 'Well Peter, I think you know what God is asking you to do'. To which Peter replied, 'Yes, but I'm not going to do it'. 'That's very risky,' said Patrick jokingly. 'Jonah did that and he was swallowed by a whale!' To which Peter replied, 'I'm hardly likely to meet a whale in the middle of Brierley Hill,' and on that merry note the visitors departed.

Two or three days later I had a phone call from Peter's wife: 'Can you come round this evening? Peter says he's met a whale in the middle of Brierley Hill.' When I went he told me what had happened. His line manager had called him in and told him to close the door. Generally his door was open all the time. His manager gave him a form to fill in – an application for the next rung of the ladder. That evening he cheerfully filled it in and returned it the next morning.

This was a public appointment and anyone could apply for it, but his line manager again said, 'Close the door'. The manager checked and approved it, but then said, 'You got the date wrong. You submitted it last month. Just change it.' 'I can't do that,' said Peter feeling very uncomfortable. 'Don't worry about it,' said the manager, reaching for the Tippex and altering the date of the application.

At home that evening Peter faced the truth. His manager was trying to do something dishonestly, and he should have nothing to do with it. Next morning he went in and asked his manager to withdraw the application. His manager resisted. But Peter insisted, and eventually his line manager called in his boss. The two of them set about trying to change Peter's mind.

But Peter held firm and in the end they gave up. 'I couldn't have done it,' Peter told me later, 'if I hadn't felt there was someone just behind me in that room.' Not long afterwards Peter did get his promotion, but he never reached the top – because before long he felt called into the Anglican ministry, and later so did his wife.

At that time I also learnt a lesson about dealing with vandals. In the manse garden we had an apple tree which one year had an excellent crop. One morning I found that the tree had been attacked and the whole crop was ruined. I was fairly sure I knew who'd done it – a boy of 12 who led a mildly disruptive gang. When I bumped into this boy a few days later, I grumpily said to him, 'You're going to be very sorry'. I could see he knew what I meant.

Thinking about it later, I realised that I needed a different approach. When I next saw him in the street I invited him to bring a friend and have a meal with us. He agreed. When the agreed day came there was no sign of him. I had no idea where he lived, but I felt I should go to an area of the town where I had never been. There was no one to be seen but I was strangely drawn to one corner of a large square of buildings and opened a door there. There was the young man and his gang sitting at the bottom of a stairwell.

I said to him, 'Have you got your mate and are you ready to go now?' 'Yes,' he said, quickly looking round and selecting one of them. We set off. The gang of younger boys trailed behind us and waited at the gate when we arrived. Barbara had prepared a meal of bangers and mash which the two ate heartily. We had only a few words with each other, but they were all cheerful. When the boys finished they rushed out and re-joined the gang at the gate. From then on I never had any problem with them, and I don't think that anyone else did.

Like most of my congregations, money was always tight. My grandparents had left me an inheritance, but by this time it had all gone to meet pressing needs in the community. However, my quarterly allowance had almost always kept us going to the end of the quarter. Only on one occasion did our money run out one week before the next quarter's allowance arrived. As I was wondering what we should do, I was asked to take a funeral, and the crematorium fee fed us for the final week.

15
A church transformed

When my time in the West Midlands was up, my District Chairman arranged for me to move to Frome in Somerset. He came from that part of the country and thought I might be able to help. The church there had a three-acre site that contained two manses, two former day schools, the superintendent minister's house, another church house, a flat and a large 1,000-seater church. It was all run by a deeply divided church council. They were all good people, but whatever one side wanted tended to be vetoed by the other so they were unable to make decisions.

When a young man suggested to me that the church could be converted into a two-storey building, I put the idea before the church council. They turned it down point blank and refused to have anything to do with it. 'If you want this, you do it,' they told me bluntly. So I called a meeting of all the church members. Word went round that the minister wanted to change the church and all should come to stop him. I put the young man's proposal to them. Then asked for questions and comments and for the next two hours I felt like a coconut at a coconut shy. Everyone derided, debunked and dismissed the idea. Asking for a vote appeared pointless.

But I felt that we should. I said, 'It's not what we want, but what God wants. Let's all be quiet for a minute and ask God in our hearts what he wants us to do.' Everybody was quiet. After a while I tentatively asked, 'Are you ready to vote?' No one spoke but the silence seemed affirmative so I asked, 'Who is in favour of this proposal?' Almost every hand started to go up in a way which reminded me of a puppet show, as if being pulled up by invisible string. Well over 90% voted to go ahead with the scheme.

Everyone dispersed again in a quiet way that I'd never known after a church meeting. People came to me for weeks afterwards saying, 'I don't know what came over me. I went to the meeting determined to vote against any proposal.' It seemed clear that God wanted it. It was now up to the church council to implement the decision of the church meeting. Yet at the next church council it wasn't even on their agenda! I chaired the meeting, so I put it to the top of the agenda, and in the end they appointed a committee of four to run the project.

Since all four were so busy that they never had time to meet, I had to communicate between them. I would go to the first and explain everything, answer objections, reach agreement, then off to the next until all four were in full agreement. This worked very well until we reached the last item. The two ladies on the committee decided that they should design the kitchen and choose the downstairs carpet. Their designs were beautiful but the headmistress of the pre-school – which used the room – said that the colour was quite wrong for messy toddlers. After six months the carpet was ruined and had to be changed.

But the plan was inspired and a triumph in every way. The church was rescued from a dire financial, physical, and spiritual situation. One elderly lady kept well away from the building until the work was completed. She then came to see it. As she looked at it in amazement she said to me, 'I was against this. I was wrong. I am sorry.'

Though it is not always fair to compare churches, it is worth saying that the building was completed on time for half the cost of a church only 30 miles away undergoing a similar building conversion. It met the physical needs of the church's work and provided a venue for many town events.

The transformed Frome Methodist Church

It resolved the division in the church council. All were united for it now.

But I was still annoyed by the ladies who took over the kitchen and carpeting and made a mess of it. When an old friend from Bolton days, a local preacher, came over one weekend, I began to explain about 'my difficulty'. 'Aren't you talking about her behind her back,' Chris interrupted. Well of course I wasn't, I argued with myself. Surely no minister would! I was just giving a necessary explanation. But next morning Chris's question loomed in my quiet time and I found my repeated attempts to avoid it quite unavailing.

But how could I possibly apologise to the lady in question? Monica was not merely a midwife, but responsible for all the midwives in the West of England, and in those days midwives were more feared even than ward sisters. However, my conscience gave me no escape, so I decided to wait until Sunday and write a note of apology.

Then after the evening service when it was dark, I would slip the note through the letterbox.

I carried out my plan, content that she wouldn't see me until the next Sunday. But next morning the doorbell rang early. As I opened the door I heard, 'Of course I forgive you, but I didn't come about that. I had a few thoughts for your service this morning, in case they are a help' – I had to take the funeral of a local sixth-former, whose classmates would fill the church – and with that Monica was gone on her way. A new relationship had been born between us.

The publicity around the new building brought new people to the church. One woman asked about the Christian life and I offered to run a course in her home with others. She responded warmly. When I told Monica she offered to help and we agreed on a weekly meeting. We decided to use Garth Lean's book, *Frank Buchman – a life*, as I realised the participants might have difficulty relating to the language used in church. Buchman expressed spiritual concepts in everyday language and was simple and practical.

When we arrived, her husband came to see what was happening, and decided to stay. His wife objected, telling us all that he was 'very difficult'. I said he was welcome, so he stayed. We had a good discussion, but when her husband attempted to speak, his wife stopped him.

After four weeks of meetings our host said that the following week she had to attend a parents' evening so could we miss a week? Her husband protested, pointing out that he could host the meeting. I joined in saying it was a pity his wife couldn't be with us because the subject for that meeting was 'How to change your difficult husband'. At this the wife said humbly, 'I see that I'm the one who needs to change.' And there was no more talk of a difficult husband.

16
A transformative new perspective

In 1992 I moved back to Stoke-on-Trent for the final eight years of my pastoral ministry. Not long after we arrived I received a letter from a friend of ours, saying that I must read a book by her nephew entitled *Who was Jesus?* I had never heard of her nephew, Tom Wright. But as I'd be seeing her, I reluctantly decided to read it. I was captivated immediately. Tom Wright, to my joyous surprise, was uncovering the historical Jesus, including his resurrection, with new tools, evidence-based research and logic that was convincing.

After reading his book *Jesus and the victory of God* I finally shed my 1950s idea of the Gospels. Set in their historical context they now began to make sense in a wholly fresh way. My understanding of Jesus and the Christian faith was transformed and deepened.

After he became Dean of Lichfield, Tom graciously gave me hours of his time, providing me with a firm basis on which to grasp Jesus' aims and purpose. My new understanding persuaded me to put Bible study at the heart of my pastoral work, and a group of us decided to meet weekly.

This proved to be one of the most fruitful times of my whole pastoral ministry as we went through Mark's account of Jesus over a lunch each week. Barbara provided refreshment with a series of delicious soups. The changes that it brought in us affected those around. One member

My daughter Jo with her husband Paul, and their son Henry

of the group had previously been known as very difficult to work with. Then one day someone commented to me that the difficult person was now quite different and a joy to work with at the office.

After we had been there for four years it became clear that Barbara was not well physically. Our doctor, who had become a warm friend, was unable to diagnose the problem. Eventually he ordered a scan. The scan appeared to be clear, but he showed it to a young colleague, who saw the early stages of a cancer elsewhere in the scan. This was just before a flu epidemic took every bed in the hospital. Providentially a bed became free and Barbara was able to go in immediately. The operation was successful, giving her 16 more years of life.

As retirement approached, I began to give thought to a conviction that had come to me some years earlier – that I should work with postgraduates in Oxford. At the time it had seemed a fantasy. I would have been out of academia for 40 years, knew no one at Oxford, and had no money to buy a house there. When the Methodist minister's housing society asked if I would be applying for a church-owned retirement house, I had gratefully said yes. I would have to live wherever a house was available.

But in the ten years before I retired, aged 70, our finances were transformed in ways we'd never imagined. Both children left home and became financially independent; we received two unexpected inheritances; for seven years I received additional payment for the chaplaincy of three hospitals; building societies turned into banks giving tax-free bonuses; for the last five years we were able to live on our age pensions, saving my stipends; and a scheme introduced by the Thatcher Government that I had taken on trust, never understood and had forgotten we had, produced a large sum. We had sufficient to buy a small house.

As we were about to do so, the trustees of Tirley Garth invited us to live there and help with their activities. For two years I researched and arranged courses on the historical Jesus for visiting youth groups and people from the surrounding area. A group of graduates who came from Oxford attended one session and were fascinated. When our time at Tirley Garth ended with the sale of the

My daughter Louise with her husband Andrew

Tirley Garth – painting by Barbara Marsh

property, our daughters urged us to buy a house in Oxford, where we would be easily accessible to them. We couldn't afford Oxford itself, but we found a good home in nearby Kidlington.

The first week we were there, the same group from Oxford pressed me to start a course on the historical Jesus. These continued weekly for the next 15 years, new people joining as word spread. They were mostly postgraduate or postdoctoral students. We stopped only for a two-week break at Christmas. Being simply a historical study it attracted those of all faiths and atheists, from many nations and opinions.

I focused on the Hebrew Bible, which reveals the Jewish mindset. It tells us that the Creator-God made everything good, in a world which humans would rule as the Creator-God's vice-regents. But evil got into the world through the weakness of humanity and stole the crown.

The Creator-God made a covenant with Abraham and his family, the Jews, to overthrow evil and set up his reign on earth. But the Jews broke the covenant and were exiled to Babylon. Yet prophets promised that one day God would put right every wrong, return to Jerusalem, set up his King on the throne, make a new covenant, and establish his reign on earth for ever through his King – a true 'son of David'. As a Jew, fully obedient to the Law of Moses, Jesus of Nazareth set out to enact this story.

But while many Jews thought the 'son of David' would achieve this liberation through military action as David had done, Jesus worked for liberation from their real enemy, evil itself, only achievable by a love stronger than hate. It meant being 'despised and rejected, suffering… crushed with pain', as the Hebrew Bible puts it. His defeat of evil would be achieved not by sacrificing others but by sacrificing himself. By loving his enemies to the end he would overcome evil's final weapon, crucifixion – torture to death – and rise as leader of the resurrection from the dead, wiping away all wrongs with forgiveness. Then he would send his followers out to proclaim his enthronement and forgiveness to all people.

His resurrection from the dead may be thought to be simply a matter of personal belief. But personal belief to the historian is simply prejudice and a brake on finding what the historical evidence is telling us. All the primary evidence that we have of the resurrection carries the characteristics of sound history. No other explanation of the event has yet been offered that works historically. Unless such other explanation is found, many historians now accept the story of the resurrection of Jesus as historically valid.

I did not engage in dogmas such as the doctrine of the Trinity. These could be explored elsewhere. My aim was simply to present the historical Jesus as he was in his lifetime, dealing only with his fellow Jews. In this light the irony today of using his name or title to divide people into parties is obvious. He was able to unite people of goodwill from any class or party who were genuinely seeking a world where, as we might say today, fairness and peace rule.

At the first session a Moldovan popped his head round the door and said, 'This isn't for me is it, I'm an atheist?' 'It's for everyone,' I said. His atheism wasn't mentioned again until he was leaving for his country ten months later. I said to him how good it had been to have an atheist taking part. 'I'm not an atheist,' he replied firmly. This, I discovered, was not just due to the course, but the course had played a part in his new understanding.

People came for very different reasons. Four weeks before returning home with a doctorate, a Chinese student came wanting to understand how such intelligent people as Oxford science professors could believe the 'impossible things' that Christians believe. She was only able to come to four sessions but returned home, her question answered to her satisfaction.

A Chinese professor came looking for evidence that 'Christian communism' was the ideal Marxists were aiming for. And one polymath Chinese who came for a term burst into tears at the end of his last session saying, 'You've made me a better man'.

I was moved by the action some participants took. A brilliant young man had worked life out when he was 16 and decided on atheism. He was now about to receive a top university degree in his finals but found himself questioning his atheism. When I was asked to give a lunchtime lecture on the historical Jesus at his college, Magdalen, he came and was so intrigued that he came to every session throughout the following year, and faith grew. After one or two sessions he decided to care for his father, from whom he was estranged. He found his father, living on the street and managed to get him into a decent home.

Another student had asked his minister a historical question about Jesus and was told, 'You can't ask historical questions about Jesus because the Gospels are not history'. He then came to the sessions till he graduated and left Oxford. After he left he wrote me a moving letter saying the course had saved his faith.

Soon after I arrived in Oxford three men joined for a session, then invited me to give a talk to the University postgraduate Christian forum. It turned out that they were the forum committee. They asked me to help them form a council of elders to assist the postgraduate society. I had the privilege of working with them and their successors throughout the period. They proved a great encouragement to me.

17
A tragic event

In 2013 Barbara – who had many times been able to catch and deal with threatening episodes of her bi-polar – told me she felt one coming. She had always been able to deal with them quickly and I expected she would soon be better. I was surprised when some weeks later she told me it was still there. We went to the doctor but her problem remained, though as she said no more about it I began to think it was over.

One evening a student who had just completed her doctorate and was returning home to Finland the next day asked for one more evening to finish the course on the book of Revelation, and I agreed. Barbara always came with me when she was well, but that evening she said she'd stay at home. She assured me she would be all right.

I was home later than usual. Barbara got up early so always went to bed early and I would slip into bed quietly

Boats at Abersoch – a painting by Barbara Marsh

without putting the light on so as not to wake her. Her dressing gown was in the living room where she always put it. I followed our usual routine and got into bed. Next morning I saw Barbara's bed had been made, but I couldn't find her in the house or garden. I phoned a friend, who urged me to ring the police.

Two sympathetic policemen soon arrived. They told me the police helicopter was out looking for her. An hour or so later they gave me the agonising news that they had found a body in the canal, and her coat and sweater carefully folded at the place she had entered the water. As the news spread, the house began to fill with our friends.

I discovered she had taken her purse with her door-key, which she only needed when I was out and she would have to let herself in. She had taken the purse into the water with her, so clearly she had no thought of committing suicide and was planning to return before I'd got home.

Our daughters recalled that their mother had read Charles Kingsley's *The Water Babies* to them and remembered that she had emphasised the little boy chimney sweep shouting 'I must be clean' as he ran to jump in the river and turn into a 'water baby'.

Barbara had told me years earlier that when she was ill she heard voices speaking to her. They sounded indistinguishable from a real voice and she couldn't tell the difference. Our daughters concluded that, just as 35 years earlier her mind had become fixated on going up a mountain, now something similar had happened, this time tragically. The coroner returned a verdict of misadventure.

For me it was a colossal, wholly unexpected loss and I was stunned for a while. It threw me back on the heart of my faith in God: the knowledge that she would be healed and safe in his hands, and death would be swept away in the day of resurrection. I felt her presence forthrightly telling me to get up and get on with the calling God had given us.

That's how she had always been in her quiet way. 'I'm not going to be a housewife,' she told me when we married. 'I'm going to be a home-maker.' For 45 years she kept her word, and provided a wonderful home for me and our two girls – and all the people who came to stay or for meals in our home, from the 13 Chinese students we welcomed at one Christmas dinner to the suicidal woman who came looking to find faith.

Flowers – a painting by Barbara Marsh

18
An author at 85

When I reached the age of 85 I should probably have stopped preaching. In one sermon I was halfway through a sentence and I couldn't think what I was talking about. I was the epitome of the joke about the Dean, 'who dreamed he was preaching in St Paul's and woke up to find that he was'. I turned to the congregation and asked 'What am I talking about?' as if to ensure they were listening. There was a short pause and Barbara began to answer – at which the congregation exploded with laughter and the crisis was over.

When this happened again I suggested to the Superintendent that it was time I retired. Since leaving college I had never written a sermon out, so I had no stack of sermons I could read. And with my aging brain I would have found it difficult to read a sermon with conviction. But I could still write.

My father had wanted to write when he retired, but my grandmother needed care, and my father was forced to

Herbert Marsh, father

My mother at the bungalow in Rhos-on-Sea we built for her and Ruth after my father died

retire early and move into her home. My sister Ruth never left home and also needed care – though she was able to work as a shop assistant all her life. These responsibilities, together with the demands of my grandparents' three-acre garden, put paid to my father's hopes of writing.

I was free of these demands, living in a retirement home in Oxford where my meals were provided. And I wanted to help make some of the best current understanding of the Bible available to everyone. Sir Ralph Waller, Principal of Harris Manchester College at Oxford University, and his staff graciously made their facilities available to me, and I wrote *A brief guide to the historical Jesus*, telling how our understanding of Jesus had changed in the last two centuries. A talented artist, Andrew Fox, illustrated it with cartoons.

Then we moved on to the gospel of Luke. When I began the seminars I largely followed Luke's account. Luke, as the one professional historian giving an account of Jesus, begins by affirming his careful research of all the evidence from original witnesses. He claims academic authority by dedicating it to a responsible public figure. Luke's is the easiest account to understand for those coming to the subject for the first time. A number of my former students pressed me to produce a historical translation of Luke, and I made a limited attempt in *Jesus Decoded*, published in 2010.

As most people couldn't understand the book of Revelation I was then pressed to make a meaningful translation. Revelation is written in codes which its readers would understand, but which for today's readers are a mystery needing unpacking. This I attempted to do. *Revelation Unpacked* was published in 2015.

While staying with my daughter in Dubai just before the pandemic a lady said to me, in a friendly manner, that everyone knows Jesus never lived. Soon after returning home I saw an opinion poll showing that a large minority of people in the UK believed that Jesus never lived. This led me to write *Jesus, Jews and Jerusalem: setting Jesus in history*. It is available on Amazon.

One postgraduate, Andrew, was so inspired by the stories of Jesus and Paul that he decided, while researching his doctorate in physics, to learn New Testament Greek. He studied the major works on Paul and his letter to the Romans, then offered to make a translation of this letter with me. He wanted to make Paul's argument and meaning clear in language appropriate for today's generation. *The world's most dangerous letter: Romans Unravelled* is now being prepared for publication.

And there is now this memoir, which I had intended simply for my grandchildren, but has stretched into a small book. I write it in tribute to just some of the many people I've been privileged to serve and work with.

When I gave my life to God, I committed the whole of it for all time and for ever. There was no such thing in my mind as 'retirement'. This was true to the traditions of my church. My father told me that in the earlier years of the Primitive Methodists, there had never been a pension fund. There had simply been an appropriately named 'Worn-out ministers' fund'. I am grateful for today's church employment pension and the national insurance pension that have enabled me to continue in retirement engaging in the work to which I was called 70 years ago.

If I am now able to make any small contribution to the future of church or society it is bound to be of a different kind. The future belongs to our daughters' generation and my grandchildren, and I am much encouraged by the contribution they are making to society. And that is true of so many others I have encountered, as this short memoir relates. They give me hope for the future.

My grandchildren, (l to r) Eleanor, Henry, Sarah, Chris and Catherine

Printed in Great Britain
by Amazon